Integrating Primary and Secondary Sources Into Teaching

Integrating Primary and Secondary Sources Into Teaching

The SOURCES Framework
for Authentic Investigation

Scott M. Waring

TEACHERS COLLEGE PRESS

TEACHERS COLLEGE | COLUMBIA UNIVERSITY
NEW YORK AND LONDON

Published by Teachers College Press,® 1234 Amsterdam Avenue, New York, NY 10027

Cover lithograph: E. Sachse & Co. (1871) *View of Washington City*, courtesy of the Library of Congress.

Library of Congress Cataloging-in-Publication Data

Names: Waring, Scott Monroe, author.
Title: Integrating primary and secondary sources into teaching : the SOURCES framework for authentic investigation / Scott M. Waring.
Description: New York, NY : Teachers College Press, 2021. | Includes bibliographical references and index.
Identifiers: LCCN 2020037068 (print) | LCCN 2020037069 (ebook) | ISBN 9780807764640 (paperback) | ISBN 9780807764657 (hardcover) | ISBN 9780807779217 (ebook)
Subjects: LCSH: Social sciences—Study and teaching (Elementary) | Social sciences—Study and teaching (Secondary) | Social sciences—Sources.
Classification: LCC LB1584 .W29 2021 (print) | LCC LB1584 (ebook) | DDC 300.71/2—dc23
LC record available at https://lccn.loc.gov/2020037068
LC ebook record available at https://lccn.loc.gov/2020037069

ISBN 978-0-8077-6464-0 (paper)
ISBN 978-0-8077-6465-7 (hardcover)
ISBN 978-0-8077-7921-7 (ebook)

Printed on acid-free paper
Manufactured in the United States of America

Contents

Preface

In *Integrating Primary and Secondary Sources Into Teaching*, I will present ways to harness the power of teaching with primary and secondary sources across various content areas through the use of the SOURCES Framework for Teaching With Primary and Secondary Sources (Cowgill & Waring, 2015; Herlihy & Waring, 2015; LaVallee & Waring, 2015; LaVallee et al., 2019; Terry & Waring, 2017; Waring, 2017; Waring et al., 2018; Waring & Hartshorne, 2020; Waring & Herlihy, 2015; Waring & Scheiner-Fisher, 2014; Waring & Tapia-Moreno, 2015). This framework is a comprehensive pedagogical approach for supporting active, collaborative, and inquiry-based learning opportunities. Through the use of primary and secondary sources, educators can simultaneously meet the pedagogical needs and expectations of today's learners and, at the same time, empower them with skills and modes of thinking to help them become more informed, active, and engaged citizens.

As context for your understanding of what is presented in this book, as well as for use in your instruction, the term *primary sources* is defined as direct evidence related to a topic of study. These are the sources that were created by individuals present at the event, place, and/or time under study. Primary sources can be any item that can help someone create a narrative, a story, or a better understanding about a subject, issue, or theme being investigated or learned. These can include documents, letters, cookbooks, clothing, scientific or mathematical equipment, ephemera, maps, musical instruments, textbooks, or literally any item directly related to the content being studied. *Secondary sources* differ from primary sources in that they are not the items or sources that were created by someone directly present or linked to the topic of study. They are items that were created after an event, by someone not present at an event, place, and/or time under study, or by an individual not directly connected to the specific topic of study. Examples of secondary sources could include textbooks, biographies, documentaries, newspapers, paintings, or any other item not directly related to the content being studied.

Through this book, I will provide a deeper and more complex look at what primary and secondary sources are and ways in which teachers can help students understand the differences between primary and secondary sources, how to utilize sources in instruction, and how to build a more complex way of thinking and approaching content, while employing primary and secondary sources to reach proposed pedagogical outcomes. I will outline the SOURCES Framework for Teaching With Primary and Secondary Sources, present explanations for each of the seven stages of the framework, and provide multiple examples of ways to incorporate the use of primary and secondary sources and the framework into the teaching of various content areas. QR Codes are provided for each of the sources and resources utilized throughout the book in order to make them more accessible (presented alongside the relevant figures or at the ends of chapters, cued to superscripts, for links mentioned in text). Additionally, I will explore the role of emerging technology in supporting each phase of the SOURCES pedagogical framework and provide varied examples of the merging of technological and pedagogical applications in the "primary source classroom."

My hope is that as educators you will find *Integrating Primary and Secondary Sources Into Teaching: The SOURCES Framework for Authentic Investigation* a thought-provoking and captivating book that inspires you to find a variety of ways to engage your students in diverse learning opportunities using primary and secondary sources. I anticipate and am confident that you will then find ways in your own classrooms to move students toward more independent, critical, and engaged ways of thinking and, along the way, will seamlessly integrate emerging technologies into the learning opportunities provided to your students. Many of the sources and resources outlined in this book, as well as many others, can be found on an associated website for this book (www.teachingwithsources.com[a]), and I welcome emails (scott.waring@ucf. edu[b]) and future discussions about what you find here in the book and on the website. Ultimately, I hope that you really enjoy reading this book!

QR CODES FOR LINKS IN TEXT

a.   b.

CHAPTER 1

The SOURCES Framework for Teaching With Primary and Secondary Sources

An Introduction

Far too often in classrooms across the United States, there is an overutilization of textbooks, lecturing, and instructional methods that focus on the superficial memorization of "facts" and the use of methods devoid of authentic and disciplined-based inquiry. Approaches such as these lead to disengagement and a general distaste for the subject being covered (Allen, 1994; Black & Blake, 2001; Boaler, 2002; Danner & Musa, 2019; Mora, 2011, Unal & Unal, 2017; Wang, 2007; Wolff et al., 2015; Zakaria & Syamaun, 2017; Zhao & Hoge, 2005). These methods of presenting content can also oversimplify the importance of various events, items, and topics, as well as the individuals present, and remove them from the complex contexts in which they were involved. One method of strengthening instruction, building higher-level and critical-thinking skills, and improving understanding and retention for students is to embed opportunities to engage with primary and secondary sources—which are directly related to the complex environments from which they occurred—throughout the learning process (Barnett et al., 2016; Hoyer, 2020; National Council for the Social Studies, 2010, 2013; National Governors Association Center for Best Practices and Council of Chief State School Officers, 2010; Waring, 2016; Waring, 2019). Primary and secondary sources are particularly effective in supplementing the student learning experience by providing multiple perspectives and allowing for the construction of more authentic and in-depth evidence-based narratives and understandings (Britt & Howe, 2014; Callison, 2013; Hoyer, 2020; Lamb, 2014; Waring, 2015; White et al., 2006; Woyshner, 2010).

Primary sources can be defined as the direct evidence related to a topic of study. These are the sources that were created by individuals present at the event, place, and/or time under study. Engaging students with primary sources across all content areas can help them foster critical-thinking and deductive reasoning skills while also allowing teachers an opportunity to personalize learning environments, making learning more authentic, engaging, and appealing for students (Bickford et al., 2020; Cummings, 2019; Lawrence et al., 2019). Making learning *active* is a critical component of student learning, as

that is how students con-
struct meaning and refine
their understanding (Cat-
taneo, 2017; McLean et al.,
2016). Therefore, teachers
can utilize both primary
and secondary sources to
expand student under-
standings and provide students with opportunities
to authentically construct

> **The SOURCES Framework for Teaching With Primary and Secondary Sources**
>
> 1. Scrutinizing the Fundamental Source(s)
> 2. Organizing Thoughts
> 3. Understanding the Context
> 4. Reading Between the Lines
> 5. Corroborating and Refuting
> 6. Establishing a Plausible Narrative
> 7. Summarizing Final Thoughts

their own evidence-based narratives, replicating methods utilized by experts
in various fields of study (Barton, 2005; Barton & Levstik, 2003; Waring et al.,
2018; Wineburg, 2010; Wooten et al., 2019).

However, simply inserting primary and secondary sources into the classroom and instruction alone is not sufficient to improve student learning and
does not adequately serve the fundamental purpose of education, which is to
"help young people develop the ability to make informed and reasoned decisions for the public good as citizens of a culturally diverse, democratic society
in an interdependent world" (National Council for the Social Studies, 1994, p.
157). For more in-depth and authentic engagement, teachers should employ
a comprehensive and structured pedagogical framework that facilitates students actively engaging in inquiry, perspective-taking, and meaning-making
in order to develop the habits of mind that are important for the rights and
responsibilities of 21st-century citizenship (Hoyer, 2020; NCSS, 2013).

I developed the SOURCES Framework for Teaching With Primary and
Secondary Sources as a structure to support teachers in their efforts to harness the power of primary and secondary sources in pedagogically appropriate
ways to construct effective, authentic, and powerful learning opportunities for
their student populations. The construction of this framework was based on
my own experiences as an educator, on feedback provided by colleagues and
students, on my own pedagogical beliefs, and on numerous research studies
and pedagogical approaches published across various content areas in numerous contexts. In the years since I first developed the SOURCES Framework,
it has been field-tested by teachers and students across the United States and
even in several other nations, has gone through several iterations, and has
been fine-tuned to what I present here.

Through the seven stages of the SOURCES framework, the learning process
is scaffolded to allow students, individually and collaboratively, opportunities
to examine primary and secondary sources, question their understandings
about an event, topic, and/or person, develop background knowledge, find
supporting and corroborating evidence, construct evidence-based narratives,
and critically analyze the learning process and findings, as well as consider

Publications About SOURCES

Waring, S. M., & Hartshorne, R. (2020). *Conducting authentic historical inquiry: Engaging learners with SOURCES and emerging technologies*. Teachers College Press.

LaVallee, C., Purdin, T., & Waring, S. M. (2019). Civil liberties, the Bill of Rights, and SOURCES: Engaging students in the past in order to prepare citizens of the future. In J. Hubbard (Ed.), *Extending the ground of public confidence: Teaching civil liberties in K–16 social studies education* (pp. 3–32). Information Age Publishing.

Waring, S. M., LaVallee, C., & Purdin, T. (2018). The power of agentic women and SOURCES. *Social Studies Research and Practice, 13*(2), 270–278.

Terry, K., & Waring, S. M. (2017). Expanding historical narratives: Using SOURCES to assess the successes and failures of Operation Anthropoid. *Social Studies Journal, 37*(2), 59–71.

Waring, S. M. (2017). Engaging history students through the use of the SOURCES framework. *In Context, 1*(1), 2–4.

Cowgill, D., & Waring, S. M. (2015). Using SOURCES to examine the American Constitution and events leading to its construction. *The Councilor: A Journal of the Social Studies, 76*(2), 1–14.

Herlihy, C., & Waring, S. M. (2015). Using the SOURCES Framework to examine the Little Rock Nine. *Oregon Journal of the Social Studies, 3*(2), 44–51.

LaVallee, C., & Waring, S. M. (2015). Using SOURCES to examine the Nadir of Race Relations (1890–1920). *The Clearing House, 88*, 133–139.

Waring, S. M., & Herlihy, C. (2015). Are we alone in the universe? Using primary sources to address a fundamental question. *The Science Teacher, 82*(7), 63–66.

Waring, S. M., & Tapia-Moreno, D. (2015). Examining the conditions of Andersonville Prison through the use of SOURCES. *The Social Studies, 106*(4), 170–177.

Waring, S. M., & Scheiner-Fisher, C. (2014). Using SOURCES to allow digital natives to explore the Lewis and Clark expedition. *Middle School Journal, 45*(4), 3–12.

questions that were not answered. The seven SOURCES stages will be discussed in more detail later in this chapter, but before considering this framework, it is vital to properly prepare students to think critically, allow them to understand what primary and secondary sources are, and demonstrate how best to utilize sources throughout the entire inquiry process.

STEPS TO PREPARING STUDENTS TO THINK CRITICALLY AND UTILIZE PRIMARY SOURCES

Students' first exposure to utilizing primary sources in the classroom typically involves being asked to look at a single source simply being displayed by the teacher or found in a textbook. If an instructor utilizes primary and secondary sources beyond simple use for the purpose of illustration or through textbook use, it typically is through the integration of document-based question assignments or similar approaches. Using these sorts of approaches as an introduction to authentic inquiry through the use of primary and secondary sources easily stifles excitement for the content to be learned and causes great frustration for many. Students typically are not prepared to think critically about school subjects and content through reading, analyzing, examining, and comparing evidence (primary and secondary sources) and often cannot even define the terms *primary source* and *secondary source*. Prior to expecting students to analyze primary and secondary sources in isolation or as a set, especially in a case when students are given the task of trying to create a narrative or thesis statement based on the evidence provided to them, students need to be able to define the terms *primary source* and *secondary source*.

One way to get students to understand the term *primary source* is to conduct an approach entitled *Leaving Evidence of Our Lives* (www.loc.gov/static/programs/teachers/professional-development/documents/Leaving-Evidence-Our-Lives.pdf[a]). In this activity, students are asked to think about a 24-hour period of their lives. While they are doing so, the students should determine what sorts of activities took place, what individuals they interacted with, what technologies were utilized, and anything else that would help somebody to create a narrative about their day. Once they have had a sufficient amount of time to think about their day, students should write down all of the evidence that they left behind during their day. This might include things such as garbage, dirty dishes in the sink, a bicycle forgotten at school, homework they completed, or clothes that were placed into a laundry hamper. Students should be given an opportunity to discuss their list in small groups of classmates before whole-class discussion ensues, and talk about specific items that they listed and what type of items might remain and be most easily accessible by others wanting to learn about their day.

Once a class discussion begins, the teacher should show how each of the items that they put on their lists is important in the construction of a narrative about the day in the life of each individual in the classroom and how each source helps one better understand the activities in which they were involved. Students can also be asked to consider how they might be able to relate the "daily" items that they are listing to any of the content being covered in the class. In one instance when I was using this approach with 2nd-graders, a student shouted out in the middle of the activity that these items are very similar to sources they discussed and examined during their recent unit on Pompeii. The nearly 2,000-year-old items they had discussed, and those that social scientists were using to develop narratives about what life was like and what happened on the fateful day when Mt. Vesuvius erupted, were not unlike the items they listed on their record of sources from the past 24 hours of their life.

A discussion of how professionals in various fields might develop narratives about various related content should be discussed and considered. Furthermore, the importance of primary and secondary sources in creating compelling and well-developed narratives should be examined.

By the end of this activity, students should understand that each of the items they listed from the day in their life is a primary source. Together, as a class, a working definition of the term *primary source* should be constructed, as well as specific items that could be considered as primary sources. Students should be asked if they might have a sense of what a secondary source might be, given their understanding of the term *primary source*. A working definition of *secondary source* should be constructed as well. These definitions can be compared to that provided by the Library of Congress (2019): "Primary sources are the raw materials of history—original documents and objects which were created at the time under study. They are different from secondary sources, accounts or interpretations of events created by someone without firsthand experience" (para. 1). Even as the students work on the definitions and on creating lists of sources, there can be some confusion as to whether a specific piece of evidence is a primary source or a secondary source. It should be made clear to them that anything can be a primary source, as it depends upon what your question is or what it is that you are trying to determine. That is why I always ask students, "What is your question?," when they ask if a source is primary or secondary. For example, a textbook can be considered as a secondary source, as the creators were not present for all of the events presented in the text, and a level of analysis and synthesis occurred during its creation. If one is using a textbook to try and determine what happened at the Battle of Lexington Green, then the textbook is a secondary source. However, if a professor of history education is using the textbook to answer the question, "How do textbooks represent what happened at the Battle of Lexington Green?," then the textbook, as well as others including narratives about the battle, would be considered primary sources. Students should continually be reminded that it all depends upon the question being asked. In other words, "What is your question?" Another example of this is when one student in a class that I was teaching inquired as to whether paintings depicting various events throughout history completed by her grandfather would be primary or secondary sources. She added that he was present for some of the events that he painted but not the majority of them. Once I asked her what she is really trying to determine, "What is your question?," this student noted that she was interested in depictions of impactful and historical events by her grandfather and others like him and stated a question around this. Because her question was focused on the representations rather than the events themselves, these paintings are primary sources. Thus, when trying to determine whether a source is primary or secondary, it all depends upon what question you are trying to answer.

In preparing students to think critically and utilize primary and secondary sources in the creation of authentic and evidence-based narratives, the next step is to ask them to analyze one source, preferably a photograph, to learn basic skills necessary to understand and learn from sources. As a typical classroom includes students with a variety of cognitive, linguistic, and intellectual abilities, a simple image for which most would have predeveloped schema may allow for the greatest number of students to find success, in comparison to using text-heavy sources or complex visuals. I would suggest that the use of an image of a classroom environment be utilized, as students will have sufficient schema developed in order to permit them to critically examine, question, and make hypotheses about what they are viewing. An ideal image for this entry-level activity is the *Daily Inspection of Teeth and Finger Nails* (www. loc.gov/pictures/item/2018678589; Figure 1.1), which can be found on the Library of Congress's website.

Proper scaffolding for the analysis of primary sources is essential to novice-level learners, so the utilization of the *Observe, Reflect, and Question* Analysis Sheet from Library of Congress (www.loc.gov/static/programs/teachers/getting-started-with-primary-sources/documents/Primary_Source_Analysis_Tool_LOC.pdf; Figure 1.2) is a perfect way to get students to begin to understand the process of analyzing primary sources.

Figure 1.1. Daily Inspection of Teeth and Finger Nails

Figure 1.2. Primary Source Analysis Tool

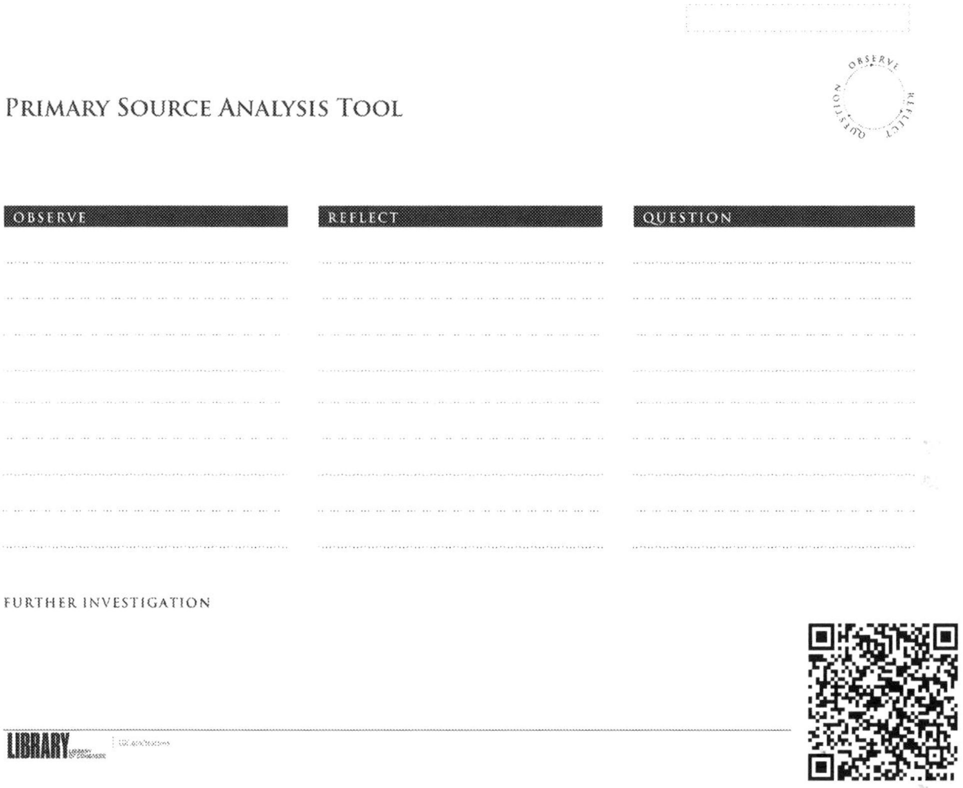

PRIMARY SOURCE ANALYSIS TOOL

OBSERVE	REFLECT	QUESTION

FURTHER INVESTIGATION

The Library of Congress also provides teacher guides (www.loc.gov/ programs/teachers/getting-started-with-primary-sources/guides[b]) for analyzing different types of sources, such as manuscripts, motion pictures, political cartoons, sound recordings, and maps. In the first column of the analysis sheet (*Observe*), students are asked to write down any items or thoughts that they can concretely say exist within the source. For example, when looking at the photograph of the daily inspection of fingernails and teeth, the students could note that there are boys and girls represented in the image, that only Caucasian individuals are seen here, or that wooden furniture is lined up in rows. It would not be appropriate to note that there is a teacher in the classroom, as it cannot be concretely determined that it is a school classroom or that any individual seen in the image is definitively a teacher and not an administrator, parent, or even a guest visiting the classroom from the local community. It often can be a difficult process for students to list only items that can be definitively observed and to make concrete and undebatable statements about them.

As students move to the second column of the analysis sheet (*Reflect*), they are expected to make inferences and hypotheses about what they think is occurring in the image. It would be completely appropriate for students to list statements about their thoughts, such as the image is of a classroom, the students are of mixed ages, the individual in the foreground of the image is pregnant, or there are multiple adults present within this classroom. As long as the student has rationale and evidence for a comment in the reflecting column, the teacher should allow them to list their thoughts; during this stage, teachers should facilitate critical and deep thinking and encourage students to consider any and all possibilities for what might be possible with the source being analyzed.

In the third column (*Question*), students are asked to list any questions that they may have about the image they are analyzing, especially thoughts and themes for which they do not feel there is a sufficient amount of information in the source to concretely determine an answer. It should be noted that these three columns can be completed in any order and it is not a linear process that must be completed left to right. A student may start with having three or four questions before even attending to an observation; however, students should be encouraged to have multiple items listed under each column header. The *Observe, Reflect, and Question* Analysis Sheet is a perfect way to introduce the use of primary sources to students at a novice level of thinking and can be equally effective with more advanced students. As they become more proficient at analyzing sources and begin using multiple sources or sets of sources at one time, more complex analysis sheets may be necessary, but this analysis sheet can and should be used with learners at all levels.

Once students have had an opportunity to carefully analyze one image, begin introducing other types of primary sources to the students, such as letters, diary entries, short video and audio clips, maps, and political cartoons, to give them the opportunity to analyze various types of sources. When using different types of sources, teachers may use the *Observe, Reflect, and Question* Analysis Sheet from Library of Congress or utilize other analysis sheets available from Teaching With SOURCES (teachingwithsources.com[c]), the National Archives (www.archives.gov/education/lessons/worksheets[d]), and The History Project (www.calisphere.universityofcalifornia.edu/themed_collections/pdf/6cs _primary_source.pdf[e]), or other analysis sheets available online from various universities, educators, and organizations.

Since a source that an individual is analyzing may not be the first, last, and only version of that source, it is important to have students engage with sources that have been edited and to critically think about how the source that is available was constructed, how it may be different from other versions of that source, and what message the creator was trying to convey to others through the item. Written works that have been edited can be powerful sources to utilize in the classroom, as students can see how thoughts of the creator changed and how even famous and notable people throughout history had to edit their work. A good source to introduce to students is an item

Figure 1.3. Image 27 of Rosa Parks Papers: Writings, Notes, and Statements, 1956–1998

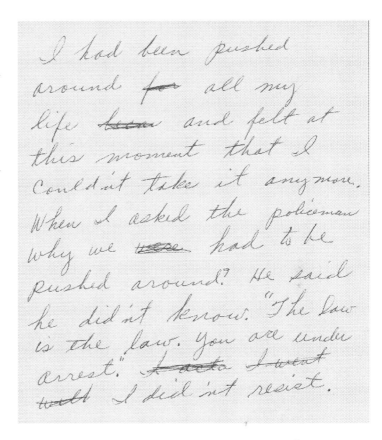

written by Rosa Parks (www.loc.gov/resource/mss85943.001810/?sp=27; Figure 1.3) in regard to the decision she made when forced with the prospect of sitting at the back of the bus. One can directly see Rosa's edits and read her associated thoughts as she explains what she was thinking at that time.

> I had been pushed around all my life and felt at this moment that I could not take it anymore. When I asked the policeman why we had to be pushed around? He said he didn't know. "The law is the law. You are under arrest." I did not resist.

Another powerful source to share with students as an example of edited work is an original typed draft of President Franklin Delano Roosevelt's *Day of Infamy Speech* (www.archives.gov/files/publications/prologue/images/day-of-infamy-draft1-page1.jpg; Figure 1.4). Students can read that he initially intended to say that this was a "date which will live in world history."

Lines were drawn through the words "world history," and above this edit is written the stronger word "infamy." Besides this monumental modification, there are many other edits found in this one-page draft. This is also a nice reminder to students about the need to edit their own writing.

Figure 1.4. FDR's "Day of Infamy" Speech

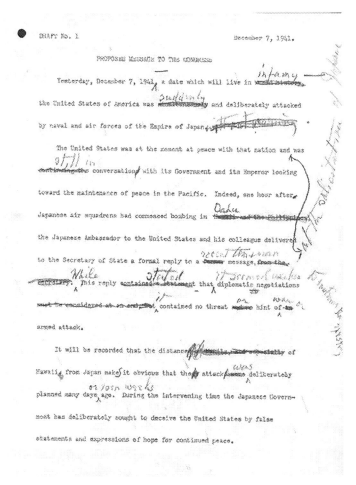

CRITICAL EXAMINATION OF SOURCES

Home of the Rebel Sharpshooter

To help students become critical consumers of sources and question each source with which they come in contact, they should be introduced to powerful images that necessitate careful analysis and thought, such as the *Home of the Rebel Sharpshooter* (www.loc.gov/resource/cwpb.04337; Figure 1.5).

Students should be asked to carefully examine the image and go through the stages of observing, reflecting, and questioning what is seen in the image. As the students respond to what they see, what they think they see, and the questions that they have, a class list can be generated on a board or by using the online tool provided on the Library of Congress website (www.loc.gov/teachers/primary-source-analysis-tool). Once a sufficient amount of analysis has been completed, the teacher should read the first paragraph from

Figure 1.5. Gettysburg, Pennsylvania. Dead Confederate Soldier in Devil's Den

the entry that accompanies the image in Alexander Gardner's *Photographic Sketch Book of the War* (rmc.library.cornell.edu/7milVol/plate41.html[f]), published in 1865–66, so that the students can read what the creator of the image thought, in his own words, when the image was captured. The students learn that "The artist, in passing over the scene of the previous days' engagements, found in a lonely place the covert of a rebel sharpshooter, and photographed the scene presented here." They also discover that Gardner noted:

> The Confederate soldier had built up between two huge rocks, a stone wall, from the crevices of which he had directed his shots, and, in comparative security, picked off our officers. The side of the rock on the left shows, by the little white spots, how our sharpshooters and infantry had endeavored to dislodge him. The trees in the vicinity were splintered, and their branches cut off, while the front of the wall looked as if just recovering from and (sic) attack of geological smallpox. The sharpshooter had evidently been wounded in the head by a fragment of shell which had exploded over him, and had laid down upon his blanket to await death. There was no means of judging how long he had lived after receiving his wound, but the disordered clothing shows that his sufferings must have been intense. (rmc.library.cornell.edu/7milVol/plate41.html)

Reading this passage significantly adds to the understanding of the image and clarifies or corroborates many of the thoughts already reflected upon by the students. The last portion of the first paragraph of Gardner's entry urges the reader to think about the family and loved ones left behind by this Confederate sharpshooter:

> Was he delirious with agony, or did death come slowly to his relief, while memories of home grew dearer as the field of carnage faded before him? What visions, of loved ones far away, may have hovered above his stony pillow! What familiar voices may he not have heard, like whispers beneath the roar of battle, as his eyes grew heavy in their long, last sleep!

With this new information, a deeper discussion can ensue, and the idea of corroborating evidence can be introduced. Students can discuss how the second source added to understandings, modified their thoughts, or made the past more personable, or in what ways more than one source can be beneficial to the process of thinking critically about the past or about any topic of study. Especially with the emotional nature of this source coupled with Gardner's narrative, students typically talk about how this humanized the process for them and allowed them to think of the American Civil War combatants as humans and individuals, not just a large mass of mechanized soldiers. After students have thoroughly discussed their thoughts, the teacher can ask if they would be troubled or upset to learn that Alexander Gardner, possibly along with his colleagues Timothy O'Sullivan and James Gibson, dragged the body across a field and set up the body, along with a prop gun, to stage the image of what he entitled *The Home of the Rebel Sharpshooter*. These arguments were made by an artist and illustrator (Frederick Ray) for *Civil War Times Illustrated* in 1961, by looking at the similarities between two different photographs captured by Alexander Gardner at Gettysburg. In 1975, historian William Frassanito decided to go a step further with Ray's observations and outline the probable process that Gardner undertook in transporting the body more than 70 yards and setting the scene to his liking. Once they have been able to digest this new information, students should take a look at the second paragraph of Alexander Gardner's entry for the *Home of the Rebel Sharpshooter* from the Photographic Sketchbook:

> On the nineteenth of November, the artist attended the consecration of the Gettysburg Cemetery, and again visited the "Sharpshooter's Home." The musket, rusted by many storms, still leaned against the rock, and the skeleton of the soldier lay undisturbed within the mouldering uniform, as did the cold form of the dead four months before. None of those who went up and down the fields to bury the fallen, had found him. "Missing," was all that could have been known of him at home, and some mother may yet be patiently watching for the return of her

boy, whose bones lie bleaching, unrecognized and alone, between the rocks at Gettysburg.

This narrative and the fact that the body was moved typically disturbs students and opens up a conversation about what one can and should do and think when encountering primary and secondary sources with which they have questions, concerns, or are even skeptical of, and further emphasizes the importance of corroboration. The idea of whether any source must depict what "really" happened and represents some obtainable Truth becomes a topic of discussion and one that is a vitally important one to broach, as well as whether utilizing corroborating information is always necessary and, if not, in which cases do they believe corroborating evidence should be obtained.

July 2, 1776, as the Date of Independence

To encourage students to think more critically about what they believe they know and about what they are told, the date of the declaration of our nation's independence can be examined. This process will help allow students to be more critical in their thinking, prepare them for Stage 1 (Scrutinizing the Fundamental Source[s]) of the SOURCES framework, and set them up nicely to begin any inquiry-based investigation. This activity should start with a listing of thoughts that come to students' minds when July 4th is mentioned. Students may reference fireworks, celebrations, family gatherings, and other visions associated with the date in 1776 when, they are traditionally told, the declaration was adopted. Images for fireworks demonstrations in Washington, DC (upload.wikimedia.org/wikipedia/commons/6/68/Fourth_of_July_fireworks_behind_the_Washington_Monument%2C_1986.jpg; Figure 1.6) can be displayed while the discussion is held. Next, the teacher should hold a conversation about the Committee of Five (John Adams, Benjamin Franklin, Thomas Jefferson, Robert Livingston, and Roger Sherman) and talk about and carefully examine the painting of *The Declaration of Independence, July 4, 1776* by John Trumbull (b02.deliver.odai.yale.edu/4b/83/4b836cfe-f3de-47b7-9899-31df7970b30b/ag-obj-69-0001-pub-large.jpg; Figure 1.7).

Figure 1.6. Fireworks in Washington, DC

Figure 1.7. The Declaration of Independence, July 4, 1776

Students should be asked to share what they know about this image, what they interpret to be happening, and how the title helps them to better understand what the painting is depicting. For more information about this painting, one can visit the Yale University Art Gallery website (artgallery.yale.edu/collections/objects/69ᵍ), where the history of this painting and a number of issues, interesting details, and inaccuracies are presented.

Once a sufficient conversation has been held regarding perceptions and thoughts about Independence Day and about the John Trumbull painting of the signing of the Declaration of Independence on July 4, 1776, the teacher should display and read to the students a letter from John Adams to his wife, Abigail, from July 3, 1776, the day before the date traditionally credited as day for the Declaration of Independence in the United States (www.masshist.org/digitaladams/archive/popup?id=L17760703jasecond&page=L17760703 jasecond_1; Figure 1.8).

The teacher should begin by asking students to determine the date of the letter and to put this into the context of what has been discussed. They should note that by looking at the top right portion of the letter, the reader could surmise that the letter was written in Philadelphia on July 3, 1776. If none state it clearly, they should be reminded that this letter was written by one of the

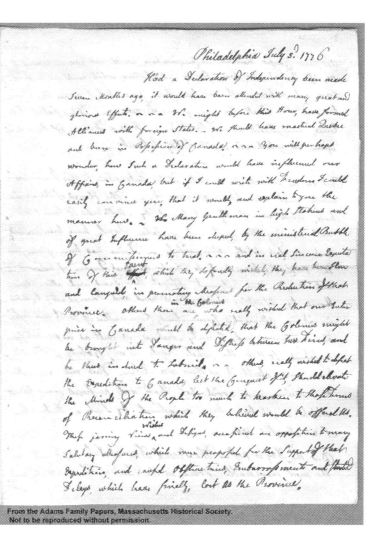

**Figure 1.8. Letter
from John Adams
to Abigail Adams,
July 3, 1776**

Committee of Five on the day before the signing of the Declaration of Independence, now known as Independence Day. The following section, found on pages 2–3, should be read to the students, where John Adams boldly and decisively proclaims:

> The Second Day of July 1776, will be the most memorable Epocha, in the History of America. I am apt to believe that it will be celebrated, by succeeding Generations, as the great anniversary Festival. It ought to be commemorated, as the Day of Deliverance by solemn Acts of Devotion to God Almighty. It ought to be solemnized with Pomp and Parade, with Shews, Games, Sports, Guns, Bells, Bonfires and Illuminations from one End of this Continent to the other from this Time forward forever more.

Students should be asked to summarize what John Adams was suggesting as he wrote this letter on July 3, 1776, and in what ways this causes them to question the validity of celebrating the date of our nation's independence as July 4 each year. They should be asked what other sources they would need to corroborate this belief, because this is a letter from just one person of the Committee of Five; what credibility this particular author lends to the validity of statements made in the letter; and whether they find this letter to be reliable. As the teacher wraps up this activity, further discussion of the Trumbull painting should occur. Certain troubling elements should be addressed, among them the fact that the painting took more than 3 decades to complete; that many depicted in the painting were not present for the signing, opposed the declaration, and never signed it; and even that some of the figures were not the actual individuals themselves but likenesses of their sons or other stand-ins. Other sources that can be shared at this point include the broadside of the Declaration of Independence produced by John Dunlap on July 4, 1776 (www.wdl.org/en/item/2716[h]), and an engrossed copy of the Declaration, dated July 4, 1776 (www.archives.gov/founding-docs/declaration[i]). Once again, students should think critically about the validity, accuracy, and fairness of utilizing a single source, such as a painting, as a way to determine what happened during an event, to characterize an individual, or to construct a narrative about any topic of study.

EVALUATION OF SOURCES

As students learn to be more critical of the sources they encounter, they should be given the opportunity to evaluate and weigh the importance of particular sources against others. They should be provided with various questions and associated sources for them to determine which source, of those available, best allows them to answer the question posed. For example, students could be asked the question, "Why were Lewis and Clark traveling west?" They could be provided with two sources: a letter from Thomas Jefferson to Meriwether Lewis on June 20, 1803, outlining the mission proposed by Jefferson (Image: www.visitthecapitol.gov/exhibitions/artifact/president-thomas-jeffersons-instructions-meriwether-lewis-june-20-1803[j]; Transcription: www.loc.gov/exhibits/lewisandclark/transcript57.html[k]) and a portion of a documentary film, such as the one created by Ken Burns for PBS (www.pbs.org/show/lewis-clark[l]), which focuses on the lives of Meriwether Lewis and William Clark. The students would need to discuss the two sources provided to them and decide:

- Which source is better for assisting you with answering the question?
- Could you use both sources?

- What are your thoughts in regard to the question posed?
- Can you construct an exhaustive narrative about the subject based on these two sources?
- If you were to have the opportunity to examine other sources, what would those sources be?

One could also present two narratives from a similar type of source, such as two articles from different newspapers about a single event. For example, one may examine two news stories about an event such as Patrick Gilmore's peace jubilee, which was held in Boston, Massachusetts, in June 1869. On June 26, 1869, the *Albany* (Oregon) *Register* published a piece (chroniclingamerica.loc.gov /lccn/sn84022643/1869-06-26/ed-1/seq-1[m]) about this gathering that characterized the event as having "from ten to twelve thousand persons. The audience was probably 25,000, notwithstanding a heavy shower." The author of this piece wraps it up by stating that at the end of the performance:

> The audience stood on the seats, shouted and made an extraordinary demonstration. The last piece was repeated by the whole mass again. At the conclusion there were repeated cheers from the audience and the performers. The building was soon vacated and every person was loud in praise of the success of the inaugural day of Jubilee.

On July 7, 1869, the *Democratic Enquirer* (Ohio)[n] ran a piece in which the author states that:

> The Mongrel party has had what they call a "peace jubilee" . . . hundreds of thousands of dollars were squandered. . . . They shouted, sang, and made huge noises with anvils, cannon, and musical instruments—all in mockery of the woes of the nation at this time.

As one can see from short sections of the two different depictions, these narratives almost do not seem to be depicting the same event. This is a good example to remind students that all sources are biased, as are the creators of the sources. Often, this bias is blatantly demonstrated in the sources themselves, but even if it is not overt, students need to remember that some level of bias is always present. It is typical for students to believe that if it is a primary source, then it must be true and free of distortion. A discussion about the inherent bias in all sources is necessary. This contributes to the argument for a need for multiple sources, from multiple perspectives, and the use of a mix of sources that both corroborate and refute understandings. At this point, the teacher should also revisit the questions posed for the Lewis and Clark sources.

As a follow-up to this, students can be provided engaging questions of interest, along with two associated sources to determine which they prefer and find to be more reliable. The Stanford History Education Group has constructed a lesson in which they provide a handout with historical questions for students to consider, such as "Who was present at the signing of the Declaration of Independence?," "What was the layout of the Nazi concentration camp Auschwitz?," and "Did American soldiers commit atrocities during the Vietnam War in 1969?" (sheg.stanford.edu/history-lessons/evaluating-sources[o]). This is an excellent resource for helping to create discerning students and to remind them of the importance of corroboration.

Teachers should discuss with students what their thoughts are regarding sources that have information missing, such as an isolated sentence, a paragraph, or an abridged version of a speech or document. For example, in the process of researching George Washington, a student may come across his *Farewell Address*. Students typically do not have an understanding of what an ellipsis—the three dots indicating that information has been left out—means and how this might impact the message being conveyed in a document. Teachers should also address other possible issues, such as transcriptions, deteriorated sources, and modern-day readings and interpretations of historical documents and speeches, along with acquiring the intended message of the original creator of a source. For example, the reading of Frederick Douglass's speech *The Meaning of July Fourth for the Negro* can be quite powerful, especially when it is read by James Earl Jones (www.youtube.com/watch?v=8tTkHJW xfP0[p]); however, because much of the speech is left out and portions of it are moved around, the reader should question this as a legitimate source to be used when learning about the past and Frederick Douglass' actual message to be conveyed. Additionally, because James Earl Jones has a familiar voice associated with Darth Vader from *Star Wars*, Mufasa from *The Lion King*, and as a spokesperson for the CNN news network, this may be confusing for students and may lead to misunderstandings about Frederick Douglass.

It is vital for students to develop skills to evaluate evidence, weigh the importance of a variety of sources to a particular narrative or argument, and understand what it is that they are seeing across diverse types of sources as well as transcripts and translations of text. This is also important because, in the next stage of the process of building students' understandings and ability, students will engage with sets of primary sources and weigh conflicting, as well as confirming, evidence against other sources focused around a theme or topic.

PRIMARY SOURCE SETS

When students become comfortable working with a single source or pair of sources, teachers should provide primary source sets (Figure 1.9) of multiple items for them to analyze. These sets may focus on topics for which primary sources can be quite elucidative and should make a topic of study clearer for students, such as is found in the following examples:

- The Seven Years' War (www.mountvernon.org/education/lesson-plans/lesson/seven-years-war-primary-source-set[q])
- Weather Forecasting (https://www.loc.gov/teachers/classroommaterials/primarysourcesets/weather-forecasting[r])
- Civil War Images: Depictions of African Americans in the War Effort (loc.gov/teachers/classroommaterials/primarysourcesets/african-american-civil-war-depictions[s])

Figure 1.9. Sample Primary Source Set

- The Harlem Renaissance (https://www.loc.gov/teachers/classroommaterials/primarysourcesets/harlem-renaissance[i])
- The Treaty of Versailles and the End of World War I (dp.la/primary-source-sets/treaty-of-versailles-and-the-end-of-world-war-I[ii])
- Truth, Justice, and the Birth of the Superhero Comic Book (https://dp.la/primary-source-sets/truth-justice-and-the-birth-of-the-superhero-comic-book[v])

As students are analyzing the sets, they are still expected to carefully *observe, reflect,* and *question* each of the sources; however, an additional goal will be for them to determine the purpose of each of the sources included, why this source set has been created, how each source is relevant to the overall theme of the set and to the other sources included in the set, and the overall significance of the set they are examining.

Lincoln's Pockets

A model example that could be introduced to the students during this stage of development is a set of primary sources created by the Library of Congress entitled *The Contents of Abraham Lincoln's Pockets on the Evening of his Assassination* (https://www.loc.gov/resource/lprbscsm.scsm1049/?st=gallery; Figure 1.10). Within this set, students will be able to see items worn by President Abraham Lincoln or found in his pockets on the night he was assassinated. The powerful thing about this particular set is that these sources were found on a person considered a great and powerful man, but when considered carefully, they are fairly ordinary in nature and used by a variety of people at that period in time or even today. This helps students recognize that all sources are useful, even the items found on an individual at any point in time. This might also remind them of the items they recorded for the *Leaving Evidence of Our Lives* activity and how these items might have seemed insignificant when they wrote them down on their list. Looking at the sources from *The Contents of Abraham Lincoln's Pockets on the Evening of his Assassination*, along with revisiting the items on their lists from 24 hours of their life, might change students' way of thinking about the "importance" of sources.

Figure 1.10. Contents of President Lincoln's Pockets on the Night of His Assassination

Teachers may introduce this in a variety of ways; however, I believe that it would be best to introduce one source at a time to groups of 3–4 students. Additionally, if possible, it is important that teachers provide the sources in such a manner or order that the overall theme or topic for the set remains a mystery until the end. This way, the students can analyze each source one at a time and continually reexamine what they think the significance of each item and the set as a whole might be. The teacher should provide a first source that captures interest and engenders conversation and speculation. After a sufficient amount of time has elapsed, a second source should be added, then a third, and so on until all the sources have been given to the students. Depending on the students' comfort level with analyzing primary sources and on the purpose for the teacher, an analysis sheet may not be necessary when examining a set such as this one. The ultimate goal for this exercise is to allow the students to see how one source in isolation does not create a proper understanding or narrative about the past. Students will see that their understandings evolve as each new source is acquired. Once students have examined all of the sources from this set and have thought about a title for the collection or a statement of the significance of the collection of sources, a class discussion should be held to evaluate various options for what the set represents. Once all ideas have been discussed, the teacher should reveal a title for the set or choose one that the students created that best represents the theme. Additionally, the teacher should ensure that all students understand what each source is, and how each is significant to the whole collection of sources and to understanding the topic of study.

Lincoln's Whiskers

Now that students understand the terms *primary* and *secondary sources* and have had an opportunity to analyze various sources and see the importance of sets of sources to the creation of authentic narratives, children's literature can be introduced as a way to serve as a basis for an investigation and the creation of unique primary source sets. An approach known as a *book backdrop* can be introduced. With this approach, the teacher shares a piece of children's literature with the students. While they are enjoying the narrative, they are asked to create a list of primary sources associated with the content presented in the story, such as sources that would allow them to further illustrate their understanding of the narrative, help to provide a counternarrative to the piece of literature, or assist in filling in missing information not fully established in the story.

A story that works well with this approach, and a favorite of mine and ranked highly by my students, is *Mr. Lincoln's Whiskers* by Karen Winnick. As the story is read, students learn about an 11-year-old girl named Grace Bedell and her effort to get then-presidential candidate Abraham Lincoln to grow

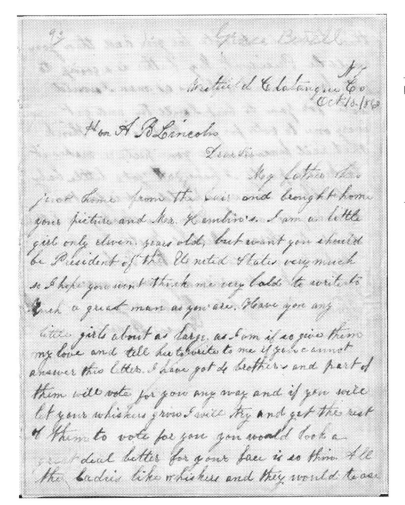

**Figure 1.11.
Correspondence
Between
Candidate
Lincoln and
11-year-old
Grace Bedell in
1860**

facial hair. Grace notes in a letter that she writes to Lincoln (www.loc.gov/loc/lcib/0903/detail/letter02.html; Figure 1.11) that with a beard, he "would look a great deal better for [his] face is so thin. All the ladies like whiskers and they would tease their husband's to vote for you and then you would be President." As the story is read to the students, their list should grow with a variety of primary sources to serve as a backdrop to the literature being shared. Among these sources could be images of Lincoln with and without whiskers, the letter that Grace writes to candidate Lincoln and his response, election ballots, and postage stamps from that time. Some might mention that they would even like the opportunity to travel in a time machine to have a conversation with Grace Bedell or Abraham Lincoln. Although this is not possible, I like to know that students think about humans as valuable primary sources and begin to consider people as sources when investigating or corroborating and refuting evidence. Through this process, students see how primary sources can help to corroborate a narrative or even provide another perspective one may not have considered. On the Library of Congress website, there is a primary source set for *Mr. Lincoln's Whiskers* (https://www.loc.gov/programs/teachers/classroom-materials) that can be shared for this activity and compared to a class list created by the students.

THE SOURCES FRAMEWORK FOR TEACHING WITH PRIMARY SOURCES

Once students have been empowered with a variety of skills related to working with primary and secondary sources, it would be appropriate to engage in more complex and authentic inquiry-based activities and investigations. Because students are afforded various ways to learn about and

The SOURCES Framework for Teaching With Primary and Secondary Sources

1. Scrutinizing the Fundamental Source(s)
2. Organizing Thoughts
3. Understanding the Context
4. Reading Between the Lines
5. Corroborating and Refuting
6. Establishing a Plausible Narrative
7. Summarizing Final Thoughts

engage with content, it is essential that educators think critically about how they frame, scaffold, and facilitate their students' educational opportunities. Thus, it is important to properly guide students and structure the inquiry process to carefully determine how primary sources will be introduced, especially because many may not have learned how to effectively or correctly engage with and analyze primary and secondary sources. Through the use of the SOURCES Framework for Teaching With Primary and Secondary Sources, students are provided a structure and scaffolding to direct their investigations. In the following chapter, the SOURCES framework is outlined for use in the history classroom. However, this framework easily may be utilized in all content areas, as you will see in examples in subsequent chapters.

In the first stage of the SOURCES framework, *Scrutinize the Fundamental Source(s)*, students are asked to analyze a primary source related to the selected topic of study. Two sources may be used if they are both deemed crucial, but for this initial stage, the use of one source is optimal. The fundamental source is the one that would be considered vital to any proper study of the topic being considered. To help scaffold the process of examining this fundamental source, the teacher should supply an essential question that will guide the entire inquiry process associated with the topic of study. The essential question should not be dichotomous in nature and should not allow for an easy, common answer; rather, they should encourage students to think critically and should necessitate careful examination and use of all of the sources provided throughout the entire process. Examples of essential questions for this sort of inquiry could be, "What historical and social impacts can be associated with the assassination of John F. Kennedy?," "To what extent did the end of slavery improve the lives of African Americans in the South?," "What are some of the events that led to the writing of the United States Constitution, and how did those events impact the content of this document?," or "To what extent did the betrayal of Czechoslovakia by the British and French in 1938 ensure that World War II would occur? (Could World War II been avoided if the Munich Pact was not signed?)" In addition to providing an essential question to facilitate the inquiry process, it is vital to provide students with other proper scaffolds, analysis sheets, and guiding questions or prompts, such as the SOURCES Analysis Sheet, which can be used with any primary or secondary source (www.teachingwithsources.com/uploads/1/0/4/0/10400589/sources_analysis.pdf; Figure 1.12). Additionally, teachers should provide students with the SOURCES Framework Analysis Sheet (www.teachingwithsources.com/uploads/1/0/4/0/10400589/sources_framework.pdf; Figure 1.13) to help them to move through the stages of the SOURCES Framework.

Figure 1.12. SOURCES Analysis Sheet

SOURCES Analysis Sheet

Know   Think

Wonder

Name_____

What do you know?	What do you think you know?	What do you wonder?

Thoughts, questions, and notes:

Figure 1.13. SOURCES Framework Analysis Sheet

SOURCES Framework Analysis Sheet

Know — Think — Wonder

Essential Question:			
Directions: While working to answer the fundamental question, answer the questions at each stage of the framework.			
S	Scrutinize the Fundamental Sources(s)	What is the origination of the source? Who wrote it? When was it written? What events could have influenced this source? What are your impressions of this source? Is it reliable?	
O	Organize Thoughts	What do you need to know to better understand the source? What other sources do you wish you had? What else do you need to know?	
U	Understand the Context	What is happening at the time when the source was constructed? Where is the location for the origin of the source? Place the source in its proper geographic and historical context.	
R	Read Between the Lines	What inferences about the source can you make that are not evident? Was there a reason for why the source was created that was not stated?	
C	Corroborate and Refute	Look at other sources about the topic. How are they similar? How are they different? Do they show agreement with the **fundamental source**?	
E	Establish a Plausible Narrative	Using all the evidence from the sources you examined, what are your thoughts about the **essential question**? What have you learned?	
S	Summarize Final Thoughts	What questions do you still have? What else do you want to know? Do you still need sources to more fully answer the **essential question**?	

For the second stage of this inquiry process, students are asked to *Organize Thoughts* associated with the fundamental source, the essential question, and any other information gleaned at this point in time. Students should ask themselves what they know about the topic or theme that is emerging and what more they need to know to properly analyze the fundamental source, as well as others to come. Additionally, students will need to critically think about the essential question and ensure that they understand what is being posed and how they might go about answering it.

During the third stage, *Understand the Context*, students are given an opportunity to think about what they know about the context related to the essential question and to fill in possible gaps in their understanding. Depending on the ability level and content knowledge of the students, this can be provided by the teacher through the reading of children's literature, viewing brief videos, reading and analyzing primary and secondary sources, listening to guest speakers, or whatever method is most appropriate and effective. Alternatively, students can independently supplement understandings with necessary information, through primary and secondary sources that they find, to form a more complete understanding of the associated context.

Now that the students have formed a better understanding about the topic of study and can formulate thoughts regarding the essential question, they are asked to revisit the fundamental source and carefully *Read Between the Lines* to interpret the rationale and purpose for the creation of the fundamental source. Students must think critically about what they know about this source presently and what knowledge has emerged since they first encountered the source. Teachers can provide specific prompts, questions, and scaffolds to assist students in this analysis. This is an crucial step in the critical thinking process; students will then understand that a source's creator(s) often had deliberate reasons for its creation that typically are not apparent from the initial analysis of the source.

Depending upon the expertise of the students conducting the SOURCES inquiry, the *Corroborate and Refute* stage can vary in structure. If students are more adept at analyzing sources and working independently, the teacher can assign students the task of finding sources that will corroborate or refute their understandings in regard to the essential question. If the students are at a less advanced level, the teacher can instead provide a set of primary and secondary sources, scaffolding questions, analysis sheets, and any other necessary information that will help them to develop a more complex and diverse understanding of the topic of study.

Now, students should be prepared to *Establish a Plausible Narrative*. This can be created in the form of a traditional paper, documentary movie, historical/cultural marker, play or skit, diary, or whatever artifact the teacher decides is the best product for allowing for assessment of each student's acquisition of the desired content. Lastly, in the *Summarize Final Thoughts* stage, students are asked to think about the process that was undertaken, the procedures and patterns of thought they engaged in that mimic what a professional does in his or her line of work, what they have learned about the topic of study and the essential question, how they came to know what they know, and what questions still exist.

Critically engaging with academic content, especially when utilizing primary sources, is a valuable and educational experience for students of various abilities and ages. It is vital that the process be properly scaffolded in order to help ensure success and, hopefully, engender interest and passion for learning. The SOURCES framework is one tool that can help teachers in this endeavor.

In the following chapters, I will present the readers with several examples of different topics that have been used in various classrooms. The readers should consider how each of the investigations might work in their classroom, how modifications might be made, and how existing curriculum might be enhanced through the use of the SOURCES framework. If teachers are flexible in thought and approach, have the proper primary and secondary sources, and desire authentic inquiry-based engagement opportunities for their students, the SOURCES framework is the perfect structure for bringing content and thinking to life in any classroom.

QR CODES FOR LINKS IN TEXT

CHAPTER 2

What Would Historians Write About Thomas Garber?

An Application of a SOURCES Lesson

In the following lesson example, students are asked to consider the essential question: "What would historians write about Thomas Garber?" The SOURCES Framework for Teaching With Primary and Secondary Sources provides the structure and scaffolding, such as the SOURCES Analysis Sheet (Figure 1.12) and the SOURCES Framework Analysis Sheet (Figure 1.13), to guide the students throughout the investigation. This lesson is presented for many reasons but mainly because this is the first example constructed and tested using the SOURCES framework, over a span of more than 20 years, and has proven to be an engaging and successful example of what authentic historical engagement and inquiry in the history classroom can and should be.

SCRUTINIZING THE FUNDAMENTAL SOURCE(S)

In this first stage of the framework, students should scrutinize a fundamental source. To begin a historical investigation utilizing the SOURCES framework, the teacher should provide students with one or, if necessary, two sources that are deemed vital to the topic of study and the inquiry to follow. In this case, the source chosen to frame and encourage engagement is a letter from Thomas Garber to Addie Garber dated August 15, 1862 (valley.lib.virginia.edu/papers/A0806; Figure 2.1) from Camp Gordonsville, Virginia (Confederate States of America). In this letter, Thomas writes home to his family to inform them about the military company that he has joined and some of his activities, and to inquire about family members and their health. Students can read the letter individually, but I believe that it is best if the teacher read the letter aloud to the class. As the letter is read aloud, students should listen for information that may be interesting, specific dates and names, or anything else that catches their attention. The teacher should lead the students through the use of the SOURCES Analysis Sheet (Figure 1.12), with careful discussion and delineation of each of the columns and questions: What do you know? What do you think you know? What do you wonder? For the first column of the

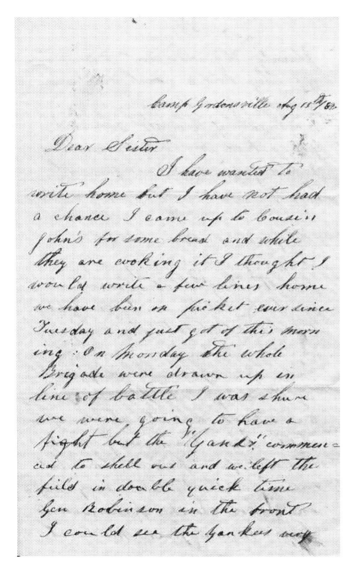

Figure 2.1. Augusta County: Thomas Garber to Addie Garber, August 15, 1862

chart (What do you know?), students will need to tell what they know about the time frame, content, or Thomas Garber from the letter that was read aloud to them. Students often mention comments about him joining Captain C. J. O'Ferral's [sic] company from Warren County, Virginia, that he is carrying the colors for the regiment, he is having difficulty managing his horse, that he was carrying a dispatch to General Jackson, and that he has seen Ash and Mike several times but has not seen Ned but once. He also asked specifically about sister Seal and mentions that he hopes she is not very sick. He ends the letter by asking Addie to give his love to Sister Seal, Pa, Ma, Kate, Nelly, and all others who ask about him. He also makes a comment about writing a good many times and putting an unfinished letter in his pocket and that once he was able to get back to writing the letter, he would learn that the letter was "spoiled."

For the middle column of the chart (What do you think you know?), students should use their own understandings and information gained from the letter to make educated guesses or hypotheses about what is happening to Thomas at this point in time, or what information that they shared means. Students have made statements that "Sister Seal" is not really a biological sister but is, in fact, a nun who is close with the Garber family. Some also think that Thomas is brave, that the Garber family might have been slave owners, and that Thomas will not survive through the end of the war.

In the third column of the analysis sheet (What do you wonder?), the students are asked to think about what they might want to know and what they wonder about at this point in time in regard to Thomas Garber, the time period, or any other information that was shared in the letter. Students often ask questions specifically about Thomas Garber, his family, what life was like for typical soldiers of the time period, and why a letter would spoil. Questions about Thomas focus on his age, what his responsibilities in the Army might be, rank, why he is fighting, where he travels during the war, and whether Thomas even survived the war. All of these questions should be captured and written on the board or projected onto a screen from a computer so that the diversity of thoughts and questions can be discussed and analyzed. This is an important step in wrapping up the first stage of the framework and can help to enhance understandings related to the fundamental source and engender interest in the topic and investigation to come.

ORGANIZING THOUGHTS

In this step, students are asked to organize their thoughts about the topic of study and to create a graphic organizer or a foldable to collect their questions, thoughts, and information learned during the investigation. A six-door organizer works perfectly for this lesson. Students are asked to choose six questions of interest and to write them in their organizer. They are allowed to use any of the questions that came up during class time, and/or they may add ones of their own. These questions may include things such as the following:

- What did you learn about Thomas Garber from reading this letter?
- What does this tell you about the life of a Civil War soldier?
- What else would you like to know about Thomas Garber?
- How could you find the answers to these questions?
- Do you think Thomas was afraid?
- Do you think Thomas missed his family?
- What do you think was Thomas's job in the Army?

- How old do you think Thomas was when he wrote this letter?
- Was Thomas killed in the war?
- Did Thomas have other brothers and sisters?
- Who were Thomas's parents?
- What was life like during the Civil War for the average family?
- What was it like to be a teenager during the Civil War?

Once students have written down their questions on their graphic organizer, the teacher can begin a discussion about how a historian may go about answering these questions. An excellent resource for determining Thomas's age or for learning more about his family is the 1860 census data for Augusta County, Virginia (valley.lib.virginia.edu/population_census[a]). This information is provided on the Virginia Center for Digital History website for a project entitled Valley of the Shadow, which is an effort to document the before, during, and after war years in a community in the South (August County), as well as one in the North (Franklin County, Pennsylvania). When initiating the search into the census records, students can learn that Thomas Garber was 14 years old when the census was conducted in 1860 (Figure 2.2). Therefore, they will be able to determine that Thomas was around 16 years old when the letter was written in 1862. According to the census data, Thomas had attended school in the past year, but the data indicate that he could not read or write. Once students learn this, they often ask how is it possible that Thomas wrote home. This is a great opportunity to get students to start thinking about various options regarding how this letter from Thomas was actually written. Typically, as a class, it can be determined that possibilities include things such as:

- Thomas wrote the letter;
- He may not have had the ability in 1860 to be considered literate but he learned enough in school to write the letter in 1862;
- The information collected in the census data was not accurate;
- The census data was entered into the online database incorrectly; or,
- Somebody who was literate wrote the letter for Thomas.

Figure 2.2. Census Data, 1860, for Thomas Garber

Personal Information

Name:	Thomas Garber
Age:	14
Order in Family:	6
Sex:	Male
Race:	White
Birth Place:	Va.
Attended School in Past Year:	yes
Can Read:	no
Can Write:	no

Location

County:	Augusta
District:	North Subdiv.

Census Record Information

Page Number:	965
Dwelling Number:	1020
Family Number:	1025

Using the information that is found here, one can then learn more about Thomas's family and determine that he is the sixth of eight family members in the "family number" 1025. If you return to the original page where you were able to search the U.S. Census for 1860, you may search Augusta County for those individuals with the last name of Garber to learn more about Thomas' family. It is crucial to use the drop-down menu for "order results by" to include the results by "family units" (Figure 2.3). When doing this, you can see that there are eight family members in the Garber household (Figure 2.4). The father of the household is Albert, age 56 in 1860, and he is a farmer who was born in Virginia.

The mother is Mary, age 48. She was born in Pennsylvania and does not have an occupation listed. There are six children in the Garber household, three girls and three boys. Thomas is the fourth-oldest of six children. When looking more closely at all of the family members, the census data records indicate that none of the family members is able to read or write. The census data records answer several of the questions that students have, including the ages of family members and other information about their schooling and literacy; however, the examination of the records often brings about new questions of interest. At this time, or when the teacher deems it most appropriate to share information about schooling and literacy rates during this time in American

Figure 2.3. Search Tool—Finding the Garber Family

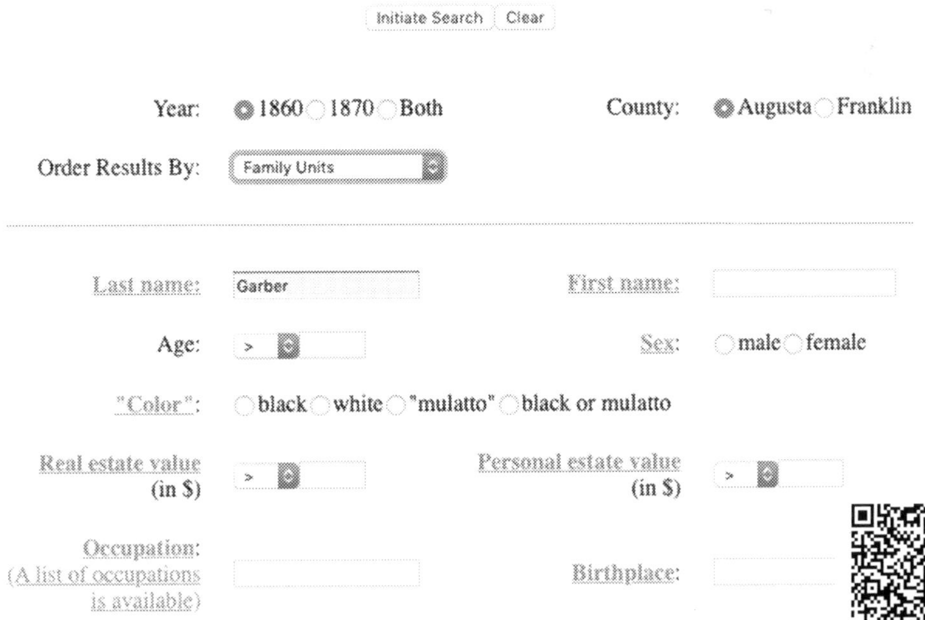

Figure 2.4. Results for the Garber Family in the 1860 Census (Family Number 1025)

1025	7	Garber	Katherine	12	Female	White		North Subdiv.
1025	8	Garber	Ellen	6	Female	White		North Subdiv.
1025	2	Garber	Mary	48	Female	White		North Subdiv.
1025	3	Garber	Asher	25	Male	White	Machinist	North Subdiv.
1025	4	Garber	Michael	18	Male	White	Moulder	North Subdiv.
1025	5	Garber	Martha	16	Female	White		North Subdiv.
1025	6	Garber	Thomas	14	Male	White		North Subdiv.
1025	1	Garber	Albert	56	Male	White	Farmer	North Subdiv.

history, one should inform the class that literacy was not recorded for any minors at this time, so in the census records, no child would be described as able to read or write. Thus, we do not know for sure, from the census data, anything in regard to whether Thomas could read and write. However, if one looks at multiple letters from Thomas to family members during this time, one can conclude by looking at how repetitive words, such as *and*, *the*, and his and family member's names, are written that Thomas wrote these letters and would be literate.

UNDERSTANDING THE CONTEXT

In this next stage, *Understanding the Context*, students have the opportunity to share their questions and tentative understandings with classmates and think about what information they know about this time period, about the American Civil War, about life as a soldier at this time, and about any other content related to the investigation. Additionally, students should be reminded of the guiding essential question for this investigation, "What would historians write about Thomas Garber?," and teachers should, from time to time, prompt the students with this question to make them think of what it is that they ultimately are trying to answer through this investigation. Situating the material within the overall context is critical to a comprehensive understanding of events, and this can be done in one of a number of ways, with the focus being on providing students with a more holistic examination, as well as the development of a deeper understanding of the content being covered. For example, reading an effective piece of children's literature can often activate knowledge, thoughts, and questions, and provide the information needed to further investigate the essential question and the unique and specific questions of interest to each student. Good options for children's literature would be books and stories that focus on the lives of soldiers during the Civil War, especially any that include main characters who are children or otherwise younger than students might imagine. For a number of reasons, my choice to share with students is *Pink and Say* by Patricia Polacco. This book has always been one of my and my students' favorites. *Pink and Say* documents the experiences of two adolescent soldiers (around the age of Thomas Garber) who were serving in the United States Army during the American Civil War, one being an African American, Pink (Pinkus Aylee), and the other being a Caucasian, Say (Sheldon Curtis). There is so much content, vocabulary, and context that can be learned from this story, and as an added benefit the story told by Patricia is one that was told through the generations of her family. One of the main characters, Say (Sheldon Curtis), was her ancestor. Documentaries, websites, additional primary and secondary sources and a class discussion about the content can be provided as well, if necessary. Such resources, whether teacher-introduced or student-selected, can be used as tools to provide additional context and information related to the topic or event under examination and used in future phases of the SOURCES framework, such as *Reading Between the Lines* or *Corroborating and Refuting*.

Suggestions for Civil War–Related Children's Literature

Pink and Say—by Patricia Polacco
Now or Never: 54th Massachusetts Infantry's War to End Slavery—by Ray Anthony Shepard
Soldier Song: A True Story of the Civil War—by Debbie Levy
John Lincoln Clem: Civil War Drummer Boy (Based on a True Story)—by E. F. Abbott
Louisa May's Battle: How the Civil War Led to Little Women—by Kathleen Krull
Nurse, Soldier, Spy: The Story of Sarah Edmonds, A Civil War Hero—by Marissa Moss
The Mostly True Adventures of Homer P. Figg—by Rodman Philbrick
I'll Pass for Your Comrade: Women Soldiers in the Civil War—by Anita Silvey
Two Girls of Gettysburg—by Lisa Klein

READING BETWEEN THE LINES

In the *Reading Between the Lines* stage of the SOURCES framework, the teacher should guide students in a process of going back to the fundamental source with their newfound knowledge regarding the source and the topic of study. Students are asked to once again engage with the fundamental source and think about their initial impressions and how their understandings, acquired since the first time that they viewed the source, have changed. This thought process should help deepen understanding, but should also encourage them to think about other questions of interest and how the investigation could proceed.

Now that the students have a deeper understanding of the lives of soldiers during the American Civil War, each student should be given a copy of the initial letter written by Thomas Garber to his sister Addie. With better contextual understanding of the time period and the fact that children were often fighting for both the United States as well as for the Confederacy, the students should be able to more deeply understand the content provided in this letter and think about what Thomas might have experienced. Students should revisit the questions that were written into the graphic organizer and think about the questions posed by classmates. Teachers should provide guidance at this point in thinking about what they have learned and how new knowledge was acquired. Additionally, they can pose questions of particular interest to the students and to this investigation, such as:

- What more did you learn about Thomas Garber from rereading this letter?
- What else would you like to know about Thomas Garber now?
- Do you wonder where Thomas traveled during the American Civil War?
- Did you consider whether he survived the war?
- Do you think that Thomas was afraid or had fears related to serving in the Confederate army?
- What are you thinking about the Garber family or individuals in the family?
- How could you find the answers to these questions?

Questions such as these focus students and prepare them to analyze their thought processes and understanding at this point in time, especially with regard to the essential question posed for the investigation, "What would historians write about Thomas Garber?" At this point, they are ready to and should consider evidence that may build, corroborate, or refute their hypotheses and understandings about Thomas, this time period, soldiers in the Confederate and Union armies, or any other questions they want to answer.

CORROBORATING AND REFUTING

During this stage of the framework, *Corroborating and Refuting*, teachers will be leading students through a process in which they are to think about and utilize primary and secondary sources that will build knowledge and/or corroborate and refute their tentative understandings or answers to the essential question provided earlier in the investigation, "What would historians write about Thomas Garber?," as well as the six questions written in their graphic organizer. For this example, teachers should arrange students into mixed-ability groups of four to five students. The students should discuss the questions that they wrote down on their six-door organizers as well as methods for how they might go about answering them. After a sufficient interval, the teacher should provide a set of letters to each group. These letters include correspondence sent from Thomas to his father and other family members, as well as letters from Thomas's cousins to the family. In small groups, students analyze:

- Asher Harman to Albert Garber, September 24, 1862 (valley.lib. virginia.edu/papers/A0808[b])
- Thomas Garber to Albert Garber, September 25, 1862 (valley.lib. virginia.edu/papers/A0809[c])
- Thomas Garber to Addie Garber, December 6, 1862 (valley.lib.virginia. edu/papers/A0811[d])
- Thomas Garber to Albert Garber, April 15, 1863 (valley.lib.virginia. edu/papers/A0813[e])
- Thomas Garber to Addie Garber, May 29, 1863 (valley.lib.virginia.edu/ papers/A0812[f])

If a teacher feels it necessary and has the time, it often works best to have five groups of students, where each group is assigned only one letter for which they are to become an expert. Students would analyze the letter to see how it might attend to the questions posed by all members within the group and found within each of their six-door organizers. They are then to provide an overall synopsis of the letter and discuss any findings related to the questions of interest with the group. Then students can be jigsawed into new groups, where each newly formed group has one expert on each of the letters. During this period of time, all of the questions, as well as any new ones that surface, should be discussed, and students should record any answers to their questions and any evidence in their organizers.

After the students have had a sufficient amount of time to analyze and discuss the set of letters, the teacher may read them a letter from Thomas's cousin, M. G. Harman, to Thomas's father, Albert Garber, dated June 20, 1863 (Figure 2.5). In this letter, M. G. informs the Garber family that:

> I have just Heard Maj T. P. Eskridge told Mr. B. Evans that Tom was killed & his body left on the Field. I have been down to see Col Davidson & Bill but can hear *nothing*. I Hope it is untrue. Come in before you say anything to Aunt or the Family about it.

At this point, students are asked what new information they have obtained and their current understandings and beliefs, especially in regard to the questions posed in their six-door organizer. Typically, someone responds that they know that Thomas is dead. It is important to pause and wait for any response from other students. Hopefully, a student will note that they are not sure if Thomas is dead. Not only is there a need for corroboration of evidence, but also there is specific language found within this letter, such as "I Hope it is untrue," and speculation rather than facts is clearly presented. Students should be asked what some of the possibilities, at this point in time, would be with regard to what has happened and the status of Thomas Garber. Students may provide thoughts, such as the belief that he may possibly still be living, that he might have in fact died, or that it might have been a case of misidentification, as well as a host of other ideas.

Students should be asked where one might find more information to corroborate the idea that Thomas has died. They might offer up several suggestions, including utilizing census data records. If not, the teacher can bring up the idea of revisiting the census data for 1870 to conduct a search for Thomas Garber in the Augusta County records. When this is completed, a result of "there were no matches for the search you requested" is provided. Students should be asked what this means, and typically, at least one student informs the class that this means that Thomas is dead. Other students may suggest that this does not mean that he is dead, as Thomas may have moved to another county, or the census data might be wrong. Students may suggest that he may have moved to Lexington to attend school, referencing evidence found within an earlier letter (May 29, 1863). As mentioned earlier in the chapter, some explain that census data records may have errors in them and, additionally, the individual who transcribed the information to the website may have made an error. These sorts of questions and further analysis help to inform the students' thinking and are important to the *Corroborate and Refute* stage in the SOURCES framework. These sorts of skills and ways of thinking are vital to authentic historical engagement but are also necessary in the navigation of opinions, stories, and theories encountered in everyday life.

Figure 2.5. Letter from M. G. Harman to Albert Garber, June 20, 1863

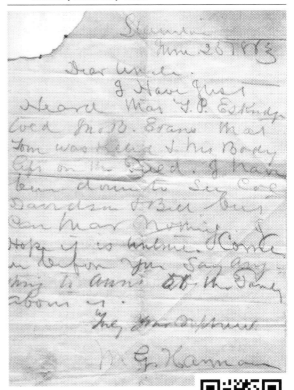

The teacher should next conduct a search looking for the Garber family (Family Number 1025) in the 1870 Census records, being sure to specify Augusta County and choose the drop-down menu so that the results are ordered by family unit. The results will show that there are no results for any Garber family members in Family Number 1025. Students should be questioned as to why this might be. Responses may include the thought that the whole family died, the whole family moved, and issues with census data reporting or transcription. The suggestion should be made that a search be conducted looking for Thomas's father, Albert Garber, as he might have been too old to fight but young enough to be alive in 1870. When the search is conducted, students will see that Albert is found but that he no longer has an occupation and that he has lost a considerable amount of land. Discussions about why a Confederate farm owner may have less land after the American Civil War should be conducted. Students should notice that the family number has changed at this point in time to 686, so they should be questioned as to why the family number changed. Responses typically focus in on the fact that the population decreased as a result of the American Civil War or that the census data collection procedures may have changed. Another search can be conducted at this point for the Garber family in 1870 (Figure 2.6). When looking for the new family unit number of 686, students will see that all the male family members, except for Albert, are no longer listed within this family unit. This brings up thoughts of whether all the male children died during the Civil War, if they started families of their own, if they moved out of the county, or other feasible options. One entry of note is the listing of a Black domestic family member named Helen. As she was not listed in the 1860 Census but is present in the 1870 Census within this family unit, it brings up thoughts of whether this family owned slaves. A discussion of how African Americans were not included in the census data prior to the American Civil War should occur. By investigating the link for Helen, students also find it interesting that she is able to read and write, as this often differs from what they had been led to believe about literacy and African Americans during this time in American history.

Figure 2.6. Results for the Garber Family in the 1870 Census (Family Number 686)

686	1	Garber	Albert J.	66	Male	White	No Occupation		
686	2	Garber	Mary J.	58	Female	White	Housekeeping	1st District	Staunton
686	3	Garber	Kate M.	20	Female	White	No Occupation	1st District	Staunton
686	4	Garber	Jane E.	18	Female	White	School	1st District	Staunton
686	5	Garber	Helen	25	Female	Black	Domestic	1st District	Staunton

After a sufficient amount of discussion has occurred, the teacher should read a letter from Thomas's cousin Lewis Harman to Thomas's sister Addie Garber dated July 20, 1863, informing his cousin that he is sending Thomas's belongings back home following his death. In this letter, Lewis notes that he "started Dear Tom's knapsack home," that he has "Tom's knife & Testament," and goes on to inform the family that he

> did not see dear Tom on the morning after he died, as we moved forward at dawn in pursuit of the enemy, when I had gotten back in the evening he had been buried by a party of his Company who had been sent to bury the dear fellow. The poor fellow suffered very little Dear Cousin, & I am sure he died as I wish to die & all other brave soldiers fighting in our most just cause.

Students are typically satisfied with the level of corroboration among the sources that have been examined. Although the idea of corroboration has been the primary focus during this stage of the Garber example, all of the sources provided may in fact have been used by students to refute inaccurate or misguided understandings and can allow students to modify hypotheses and thoughts throughout the entire stage.

At this point, some students would like to have further evidence to be fully satisfied with the notion that Thomas has died. To help with this, the teacher may reference a newspaper article from the *Staunton Vindicator*, dated July 3, 1863 (valley.lib.virginia.edu/newspapers[g]). In the article, one may read that "Thomas Garber of Augusta County was wounded in fighting in Upperville and has since died." Additional research can be conducted on the Battle of Upperville to learn more about this battle and the progress of Thomas's unit.

To help students think critically, the teacher may ask students why one would find a newspaper clipping about Thomas Garber in the *Staunton Vindicator* from May 11, 1866 (valley.lib.virginia.edu/news/rv1866/va.au.rv.1866. 05.11.xml#03[h]). Students typically come up with ideas such as that this could be a newspaper article about another Thomas Garber, that perhaps he really did not die, or that there might be a memorial that has been posthumously dedicated to Thomas. After discussion has occurred about this new piece of evidence, students should be given the opportunity to view the rest of the text of the article:

> The remains of our gallant young townsman, Thos. M. Garber, youngest son of Albert J. Garber, Esq., color bearer of the 12th Virginia Cavalry, who fell mortally wounded in a cavalry engagement near Upperville, Va., were brought to Staunton on Tuesday week and re-interred in Thornrose Cemetery.

If there were concerns about the validity of the narrative that has been constructed to this point, this last piece of evidence typically eliminates any doubt.

Figure 2.7. The Army of the Potomac—Skirmish Near Upperville—Ashby's Gap in the Distance

Two final primary sources should be shared with the students in order to help with answering any additional questions and to build a deeper narrative about the life of Thomas Garber. The first is an illustration by Arthur R. Waud in the *Harper's Weekly* periodical (Figure 2.7). On July 11, 1863, there is the inclusion of an image from the "Battle Near Upperville." The caption reads:

> On page 445 we reproduce a sketch by Mr. A. R. Waud, illustrating THE BATTLE NEAR UPPERVILLE, Ashby's Gap in the distance. The square inclosure is called the vineyard; on the right on the rise is a stone-wall; against this a charge was made, the men returning to form again a little to the left. On the extreme left five rebel regiments came out with their large flags to charge our men before they could form, but the First and Sixth regulars, sweeping round the hill, charged upon them while the band played Hail Columbia.

The teacher should walk students through the thought process around what Thomas's role was in his regiment (color bearer) and lead them to understand that the last moments of Thomas's life were recorded in the image drawn by Arthur Waud and that he even makes mention that the "regiments came out with their large flags to charge our men." The sharing of this source, and even typing about it now, always brings a "goose bumps" moment for me, as it still amazes me that this drawing exists and that we have a depiction and caption about the final moments of life for Thomas Garber.

The final source to be shared is an autobiography by Charles O'Ferrall (Figure 2.8) entitled "Forty Years of Active Service." As the investigation can take on a life of its own and an end may be difficult to find if students were to consider all of the possible questions and avenues and the various paths on which the inquiry and questioning could travel, this source was chosen to be the last as a way to wrap up this investigation. It brings the inquiry back full circle to the initial fundamental source, as Charles O'Ferrall is mentioned by Thomas in his letter to his sister on August 15, 1862. If needed, the students should be reminded that in the initial letter that was read, Thomas mentions that he has "joined Capt. C. J. O'Ferral's [sic] from Warren County Va." Thus, this book is written by Thomas's commanding officer and was published in 1904. On pages 79–80 of the autobiography (https://play.google.com/books/reader?id=b5S7Vu8FvUQC&hl=en&pg=GBS.PA79), Charles writes:

Figure 2.8. Forty Years of Active Service

Forty years of active service

Charles Triplett O'Ferrall

For some time prior to the Battle of Upperville the color-bearer of the Twelfth Cavalry was Tom Garber, a member of my company. Colonel Harman was Tom's cousin, and when Tom came to the regiment he asked his advice as to what company he should join, and the Colonel told him he thought Company I would suit him, so he enlisted in my company.

It did not take me long to determine of what mental he was made. In a fight he was in his element, and the hotter it was the better he liked it. He was only seventeen years of age, yet he was over six feet in height, splendidly built, and much more mature every way than most boys of his age. He had been raised in the saddle and was a superb rider. A vacancy occurred in the color sergeancy of the regiment—how it occurred I do not now remember, and Tom applied for the position and it was given to him, and never in any war, on any field, were the colors of an army more grandly and heroically borne.

He entered the charge at Upperville in the van, with his colors streaming in the breezes above his head as he charged down the field to the stone fence. There under the rain of lead he stood waving the stars and bars until just as I was shot, when he reeled in his saddle, and still clinging to his flag staff he fell to the ground dead. He was the brother of Major A. H. Garber, of Richmond, whose record as the commander of Garber's battery is too well known to require any encomiums from me. Of all the brave and intrepid boys whom it was my pleasure and privilege to observe during four years of strife I never saw one who was superior of

Tom Garber; and as brave and dashing as our calvalrymen were generally, I do not detract from them when I declare that I recall comparatively few who were his equals, taking him all and all. He rests in Thornrose Cemetery at Staunton, beneath the sod of old Augusta, and while she can boast of many gallant sons, she had none more gallant than the young color-bearer of the Twelfth Calvary who yielded up his life at Upperville.

This statement from Thomas's superior officer is a powerful and concrete way to conclude the inquiry and serves as a testament to the kind of person Thomas was. This is a captivating narrative and one that can nicely wrap up the corroborating and refuting stage of the investigation.

ESTABLISHING A PLAUSIBLE NARRATIVE

During the *Establishing a Plausible Narrative* stage of the SOURCES framework, students should think about the essential question, "What would historians write about Thomas Garber?," the investigation that ensued, and how they might be able to best answer the question that was to frame the inquiry process. This narrative can come in a variety of formats and should serve as an excellent opportunity for the teacher to assess the students' understanding and ability to think historically and to formulate and propose an evidence-based response to a critical question of interest. In order to assess the students' understanding of who Thomas was and the life that he lived during the American Civil War, they should create whatever assessment piece is deemed appropriate by the teacher or, if appropriate, by the students themselves. A good option is for the students to create a historical marker for Thomas Garber at the location of the Battle of Upperville or in his hometown. They could also write a letter to a local historical society outlining why Thomas Garber should be remembered, create a documentary film, write a piece of children's literature or a graphic novella, or whatever option is best to ascertain that the students acquired the desired information from the lesson. Students should also use any and all resources available, such as all of the sources used in the investigation and other Garber family letters found on the *Valley of the Shadow* website (valley.lib.virginia.edu/VoS/personalpapers/collections/augusta/garber.html[i]). This opportunity to establish an original and evidence-based narrative is extremely important, not only for the historical inquiry process but also as a process necessary for civic engagement and agency, as students need these skills in everyday life to be able to critically examine sources and perspectives and develop a response to a question, problem, or position posed to them. This leads them into the final stage, in which metacognitive awareness and thinking are employed.

SUMMARIZING FINAL THOUGHTS

In this final stage, students are asked to revisit the inquiry process and think about what they have learned from the Garber lesson, explicitly focusing on the questions that they posed in the *Organizing Thoughts* stage of the framework at the beginning of the investigation. Students should be asked to consider:

- How do I know what I know?
- What do historians do?
- Did I replicate what historians might do?
- What questions still exist?
- Is it okay that questions still exist?
- How might I answer questions that still exist?

This thinking and subsequent conversation are building upon everything that students encountered, but they should specifically attend to what they entered on the analysis sheet (Figure 1.12) utilized at the beginning of the inquiry, and on to the six-door graphic organizer. The students should be encouraged to think about what they still wonder, want to know, or answer. These thoughts should be recorded and discussed further.

CONCLUSION

Through the utilization of the SOURCES Framework for Teaching with Primary and Secondary Sources, students are taken through an authentic historical inquiry process, focusing on an American Civil War soldier possibly not far off in age from them. Students are able to engage with the past and answer their unique questions with real sources from the time period. They are able to go through thought processes similar to those used by experts in social sciences and history and, at the same time, learn and practice skills vital to being critically thinking and engaged citizens in society. In fact, these students should be considered as junior historians and given additional opportunities to engage in further authentic history inquiry. Their skills, knowledge, and critical-thinking abilities will only be enhanced. In the example found in the next chapter, students move from someone obscure like Thomas Garber to one of the founding brothers and our first president, George Washington, and examine and assess his plan, as Commander of the Continental Army, to attack Princeton at the beginning of 1777.

QR CODES FOR LINKS IN TEXT

a. b. c. d. e.

f. g. h. i.

CHAPTER 3

Assessing General Washington's Plan to Attack Princeton at the Beginning of 1777

An Application of the SOURCES Framework

For my part my Lucy I look up to Heaven & most devoutly thank the great Governor of the Universe for producing this turn in our affairs of America— & this sentiment I hope will so prevail on the Hearts of the people . . .

Henry Knox to Lucy Knox

In the opening statement made by one of General George Washington's most trusted advisors and officers—and his eventual choice as the first Secretary of War—Henry Knox states the vital importance of the Battle of Princeton to the morale of those on the home front and to the success of the efforts for an independent American nation. In the following investigation scaffolded by the SOURCES Framework for Teaching With Primary and Secondary Sources, students are asked to assess the decisions made by General Washington and his choice to attack Princeton at the beginning of 1777, not only through the sources provided but in light of the statement made by Henry Knox about the importance of this battle.

As the end of 1776 drew near, control of the colonies in North America hung in the balance. General William Howe, the British commanding officer, decided to suspend military operations until the spring. In the Continental Army, morale was low, and, to make matters worse, the enlistment term for most of the Continentals was due to expire at midnight on December 31. General George Washington decided that "desperate diseases require desperate Remedies" (Washington, December 20, 1776, p. 382) and determined that the time for an attack was now, and Trenton, New Jersey, was the perfect location for it. After a decisive victory at Trenton over the Hessians, many began to consider General Washington a truly brilliant leader (Wertenbaker, 1922). Initially, Washington determined that further operations at that time would not be wise and retreated across the Delaware River (Washington, December 27, 1776). With this critical victory and after heavy solicitation from Washington and others, many of Washington's veteran soldiers reenlisted.

After hearing of the rebel victory at Trenton, General Howe readied his 8,000 troops to combat the assorted group of 5,000 men assembled by Washington, who had once again crossed the Delaware River and occupied Trenton. Howe dispatched General James Grant with all of the available troops to Princeton. On January 2, 1777, General Cornwallis left Princeton with more than 5,000 men to push back the rebels to the Delaware River and to destroy them there. In Princeton, Colonel Mawhood was left with three regiments of infantry and light horse and was given orders to follow on the next day. At this time, Washington sent forward Colonel Joseph Reed, with 12 men, on a reconnaissance expedition to determine the intentions of General Howe, as well as to assess current troop strength. Reed determined that the British forces were numerous and that the outposts were heavily defended; however, on his return trip to Trenton, he was able to surprise a detachment of 12 British soldiers on a scouting mission. From the interrogation of these prisoners, Washington was able to determine that Cornwallis was rapidly approaching with a large force and that he must prepare for the worst.

In the late hours of January 2, 1777, Washington brought together a war council to determine the proper course of action. There were three possible options that Washington posed: stand and fight; retreat down the Delaware River and attempt to cross into Pennsylvania; or travel south around the British flank and move up toward Princeton (Ketchum, 1973). Washington, and others, believed that if the army were to remain in its present position, it most certainly meant a disastrous defeat and would possibly risk the entire Revolutionary cause. To retreat to the Delaware River would lead to inevitable surrender (Wertenbaker, 1922). It was thought that the only option was to escape around the British left flank and move up the New Jersey highlands. Although this could be a risky maneuver, Washington knew that staying put would be costly, if not completely detrimental, and also wanted to avoid the appearance of retreat. Following days of warmer weather, which made the ground marsh-like and travel difficult, the Continental Army got lucky. Temperatures steadily fell through the night, and the ground began to freeze. This "providential change of weather" (Stryker, 1898, p. 273), as Washington would later describe it, allowed the option of traveling around the British flank, through Princeton, and on toward New Brunswick more feasible and, additionally, would bring the prospect of procuring much-needed supplies. Ultimately, Washington determined that the most prudent decision was to take his 6,000 troops and proceed toward Princeton in the early hours of January 3, 1777, before continuing north toward New Brunswick.

Before this was to be done, Washington decided that he would try to lead Cornwallis into thinking that he and his troops had remained in camp at Assunpink (Trenton) by ordering his men to construct earthwork defenses there and by doubling the numbers of guards posted. When it was time to leave, fires were left burning, and about 500 men and two cannons stayed behind in order to help deceive Cornwallis into thinking that the entire army remained. Any details that would add to the charade of a defensive stance were considered and, if possible, employed. The troops left behind in Assunpink were ordered to leave just before dawn and follow as expeditiously as possible. The ultimate plan was for Washington and his men to take Princeton and eventually move on to New Brunswick, capturing any enemy combatants and supplies along the way. There is debate as to whether the decision to leave the fires burning and using the flanking maneuver to move past the oncoming British troops was Washington's alone; however, as commander in chief, he deserves full credit for what may have been the most brilliant strategy conceived during the Revolutionary War (Wertenbaker, 1922).

One of the primary sources that assisted Washington in deciding to prepare this deception and to move toward Princeton, around the British left flank, was a reconnaissance map that was provided to Washington by Colonel John Cadwalader (www.loc.gov/item/gm71000925; Figure 3.1). This spy map provided an overview of the area surrounding Princeton, as well as the strength, numbers, and positions of the British and their batteries. Specifically, it showed the weakest point at which to attack the enemy, as well as how to reach it and the best methods for taking advantage of its limitations. Today the Cadwalader map is considered a somewhat inaccurate, but highly valuable, map that significantly helped General Washington plan for the success of that campaign (Library of Congress, n.d.). This map, *Plan of Princeton, Dec. 31, 1776,* allows students to better conceptually understand and engage with the content associated with the Battle of Princeton.

Figure 3.1. Plan of Princeton, December 31, 1776

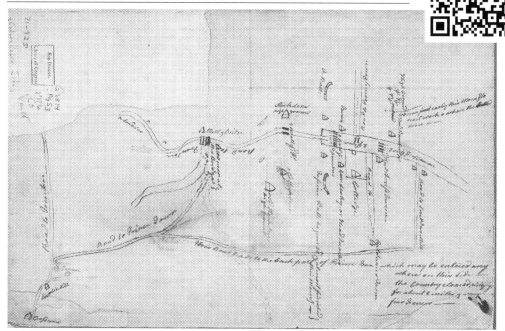

SCRUTINIZING THE FUNDAMENTAL SOURCE(S) AND ORGANIZING THOUGHTS

In the first stage of the SOURCES framework, *Scrutinizing the Fundamental Source(s)*, students are asked to analyze the Cadwalader spy map and associated letter (www.loc.gov/item/mgw446309/?loclr=blogmap; Figure 3.2; transcription available at founders.archives.gov/documents/Washington/03-07-02-0386[a]) that was sent to General Washington from Colonel Cadwalader on December 31, 1776 using the What do you know?, What do you think you know?, and What do you wonder? analysis sheet (Figure 1.12). If deemed necessary, specific questions can be used to help guide in the analysis of maps for key elements that include:

1. What do you know? Have students identify and note details.
   a. Describe what you see.
   b. What do you notice first?
   c. What graphical elements do you see?
   d. What place or places does the map show?
   e. What, if any, words do you see?
   f. What on the map looks strange or unfamiliar?

Figure 3.2. John Cadwalader to George Washington, December 31, 1776

2. What do you think you know? Encourage students to generate and test hypotheses about the source.
   a. Why do you think this map was made?
   b. Who do you think the audience was for this map?
   c. What does this map tell you about what the people who made it knew and what they didn't?
   d. If this map was made today, what would be different?

3. What do you wonder? Have students ask questions to lead to more observations and reflections.

    a. What do you wonder about?

    b. Who? What? When? Where? Why? How?

    c. What more do you want to know, and how can you find out?

In the accompanying letter from Cadwalader to Washington, students can gain additional information about the British troop numbers and actions. They can be provided guiding questions and the SOURCES Analysis Sheet (Figure 1.12) to better analyze and understand the letter. Additionally, teachers' guides and primary source analysis tools from the Library of Congress (www.loc.gov/programs/teachers/getting-started-with-primary-sources/guides[b]) may be helpful. To better understand the map, a video provided by the Library of Congress, *How to Get into Princeton* (www.loc.gov/item/myloc19[c]), could be viewed. This video includes a narration by Library of Congress historian John Hebert in which he clearly describes details of the letter and the importance of this particular map. The video complements the Cadwalader map and letter.

ORGANIZING THOUGHTS AND UNDERSTANDING THE CONTEXT

During the second (*Organize Thoughts*) and third stages (*Understand the Context*) of the SOURCES framework, students consider what they know about the fundamental source(s) and related content. These stages will typically be utilized independently; however, for this lesson, and for the structure of this chapter, they will be presented together. Throughout the investigation, students should focus on the following essential question: "In your estimation, to what extent was the campaign on Princeton a prudent and successful one?"

To begin, students need to organize their thoughts and understanding as it relates to the American Revolution, General George Washington, Princeton, New Jersey, and the process undertaken in the creation of the United States of America as a nation independent of the British Empire. Next, teachers should instruct students to complete background work associated with the fundamental source and essential question to better understand the historical context related to the time period and historic event under study. In order to assist students in better understanding this particular source and the events leading up to the Battle of Princeton, they can be provided with a variety of primary and secondary sources to develop a deeper understanding of the geography, time frame, and historical context, as well as Washington's decision to move his troops toward Princeton.

Imagery can be powerful and extremely helpful in assisting students to better understand the context of an historic event. Two images in particular, *Washington Crossing the Delaware: On the Evening of Dec 25th, 1776, Previous to the Battle of Trenton* (www.loc.gov/pictures/item/2002698169[d]) and *Washington Passing the Delaware, Evening Previous to the Battle of Trenton, Dec. 25th, 1776* (www.loc.gov/pictures/item/98501385[e]), can bolster their understanding and paint a picture illustrating the conditions, weather, and logistics of moving more than 5,000 men and associated supplies; however, any inaccuracies in these sources should also be discussed.

Additionally, many letters can be utilized to help students, especially these available from the Library of Congress:

- *George Washington to Alexander McDougall, December 28, 1776;* The George Washington Papers at the Library of Congress, 1741–1799. Available at www.loc.gov/item/mgw446294[f]
- *George Washington to William Maxwell, December 28, 1776;* The George Washington Papers at the Library of Congress, 1741–1799. Transcript available at founders.archives.gov/documents/Washington/03-07-02-0367[g]
- *George Washington to Morristown, New Jersey, Detachment Commanding Officer, December 30, 1776;* The George Washington Papers at the Library of Congress, 1741–1799. Available at www.loc.gov/item/mgw3b.002[h]
- *George Washington to Continental Congress Governing Committee, January 1, 1777;* The George Washington Papers at the Library of Congress, 1741–1799. Available at www.loc.gov/item/mgw446332[i]

Several websites that can help students fill in gaps in understanding historical context include: *History*'s site for *Battles of Trenton and Princeton* (www.history.com/topics/american-revolution/battles-of-trenton-and-princeton[j]), PBS's site *George Washington: Founding Father* (www.pbs.org/foundingfather[k]), and the State of New Jersey's *Hangout NJ* site for the Battle of Princeton (www.state.nj.us/hangout_nj/200401_princeton_p2.html[l]). Books that may be of interest to help teachers build contextual knowledge include David Hackett Fischer's *Washington's Crossing* (2004), Richard Ketchum's *The Winter Soldiers: The Battles for Trenton and Princeton* (1973), and William Stryker's *The Battles of Trenton and Princeton* (1898).

READING BETWEEN THE LINES

Now that the students have a better understanding of the context, in the fourth stage, *Read Between the Lines*, they are asked to revisit the fundamental source(s). At this stage of the SOURCES framework, students should have a better understanding of the importance of the Cadwalader map and be able to more clearly consider its significance and the impact that this source had on the decisions that needed to be made by General Washington. They should be able to gain a better understanding of the area surrounding Princeton, and since many may not have previously considered the position of the British and their batteries as well as the strength and numbers of the enemy, this map, along with the new contextual understanding, allows students to better comprehend why General Washington determined the location for where to attack the enemy, where the British forces might be the weakest, and the best way to turn the British limitations into advantages for the American army. If necessary, additional guiding questions and analysis sheets can be provided for the novice-level learners.

CORROBORATING AND REFUTING

For the fifth stage (*Corroborate and Refute*), students are asked to conduct research to find sources that provide corroborating evidence and/or those that may refute an argument that they are constructing in response to the essential question guiding the inquiry, "In your estimation, to what extent was the campaign on Princeton a prudent and successful one?" Teachers can scaffold this process as much or as little as needed. As students grapple with how to answer the essential question, they can be provided a list of possible sources for reference, or they can conduct research on their own if they have already been properly instructed on how to successfully do this. Additionally, students who have been properly trained to think critically and to utilize sources in this manner will not see this as a leading question and will feel compelled to respond along an entire spectrum of thoughts and responses.

Numerous sources can be provided to students as they construct a response to the essential question. One of the sources that may help students to combat historical presentism is the painting entitled *Washington at Princeton* (www.loc.gov/pictures/item/2003671527; Figure 3.3).

Figure 3.3. Washington at Princeton, January 3, 1777

Often, novice historians place the historical events they are studying in a present-day context. Although there can be some historical inaccuracies inherent within images, paintings and other images can combat this urge to see the past through a present-day lens, a practice also known as historical presentism. Paintings, photographs, and other visuals provide students with sources that can be quite powerful when used for comparison, corroboration, and consideration, especially when conducting an investigation exclusively utilizing written and other nonvisual sources. Additional images that can be helpful with the development of contextual understanding of what military maneuvers and forces looked like in the late 1700s, specifically Washington's army at Princeton, are *Washington at Princeton January 3d. 1777* (Figure 3.4), published by Currier and Ives, and *The Battle at Princeton* (Figure 3.5), by John Trumbull.

Although the Cadwalader map is vital to grappling with Washington's understanding of the British forces present in Princeton, it does not provide an overview of the area between and surrounding Trenton and Princeton. The *Plan of the Operations of General Washington Against the King's Troops in New*

Figure 3.4. Washington at Princeton, January 3rd, 1777

Library of Congress Prints and Photographs Division. Available at loc.gov/pictures/item/2002698168

Jersey (Figure 3.6) is a map showing the area from Newtown, Pennsylvania, to Kingston, New Jersey, with routes of British and American forces.

If a different perspective of the "Affair of Princeton" is desired, one can examine the map constructed by Henry Schenck Tanner in 1816 (graphicarts.princeton.edu/2014/05/17/affair-of-princeton-january-3-1777ᵐ).

Figure 3.5. The Battle at Princeton

Library of Congress Prints and Photographs Division. Available at www.loc.gov/pictures/item/98501341

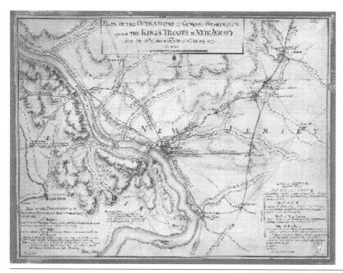

Figure 3.6. Plan of the Operations of General Washington Against the King's Troops in New Jersey, from the 26th of December 1776 to the 3rd of January 1777

Library of Congress Geography and Map Division. Available at www.loc.gov/item/gm71000654

Furthermore, specific letters that can provide details in answering the essential question are ones written on January 5, 1777 from George Washington to the Continental Congress (Figure 3.7), Israel Putnam (Figure 3.8), William Heath (Figure 3.9), and the New York Committee of Safety (founders.archives. gov/documents/Washington/03-07-02-0414[n]).

From these sources one can find excerpts that may be useful in attending to the creation of an overall narrative and in providing evidence in answering the essential question. These include passages such as Washington's overall thoughts summarized in his statement to Israel Putnam:

> Fortune has favord us in an attack on Princeton. . . . march't for Princeton which we reacht next morning by about Nine oClock—There was three Regiments Quarterd there of British Troops—which we Attackt and Routed. . . . As we have made two successful Attacks upon the Enemy—by way of surprise—they will be pointed with resentment and if there is any possibillity of retalliateing will Attempt it. (Washington, 1777)[o]

Figure 3.7. George Washington to Continental Congress, January 5, 1777

In another source, Washington was notified by John Hancock that:

> Congress are infinitely anxious to hear the Event; and humbly hope, that Victory has declared in Favour of those, whose sacred Cause should inspire them with Ardour, on every solemn Appeal to that Being, who hateth all Injustice, Tyranny, and Oppression. (Hancock, 1777)[p]

Washington also received a letter from the Continental Congress Executive Committee that informed him that "We waited with Impatience to learn the consequence of your late movements and have been highly gratified" (Continental Congress Executive Committee, 1777, para. 1). To gather additional sources of information, students can perform a search of *The George*

The George Washington Papers at the Library of Congress, 1741–1799. Available at www.loc.gov/item/mgw446345

Figure 3.8. **George Washington to Israel Putnam, January 5, 1777**

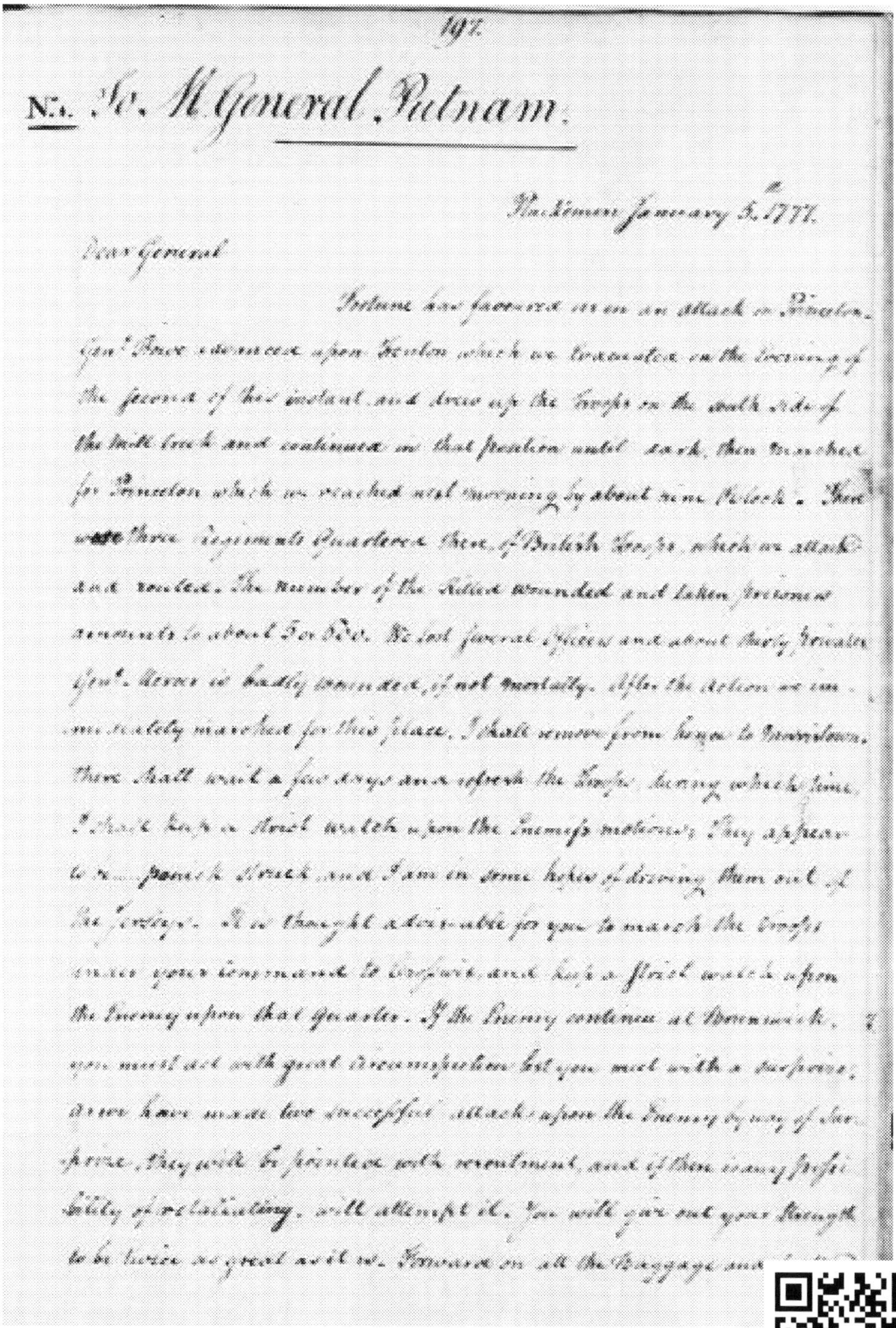

Figure 3.9. George Washington to William Heath, January 5, 1777

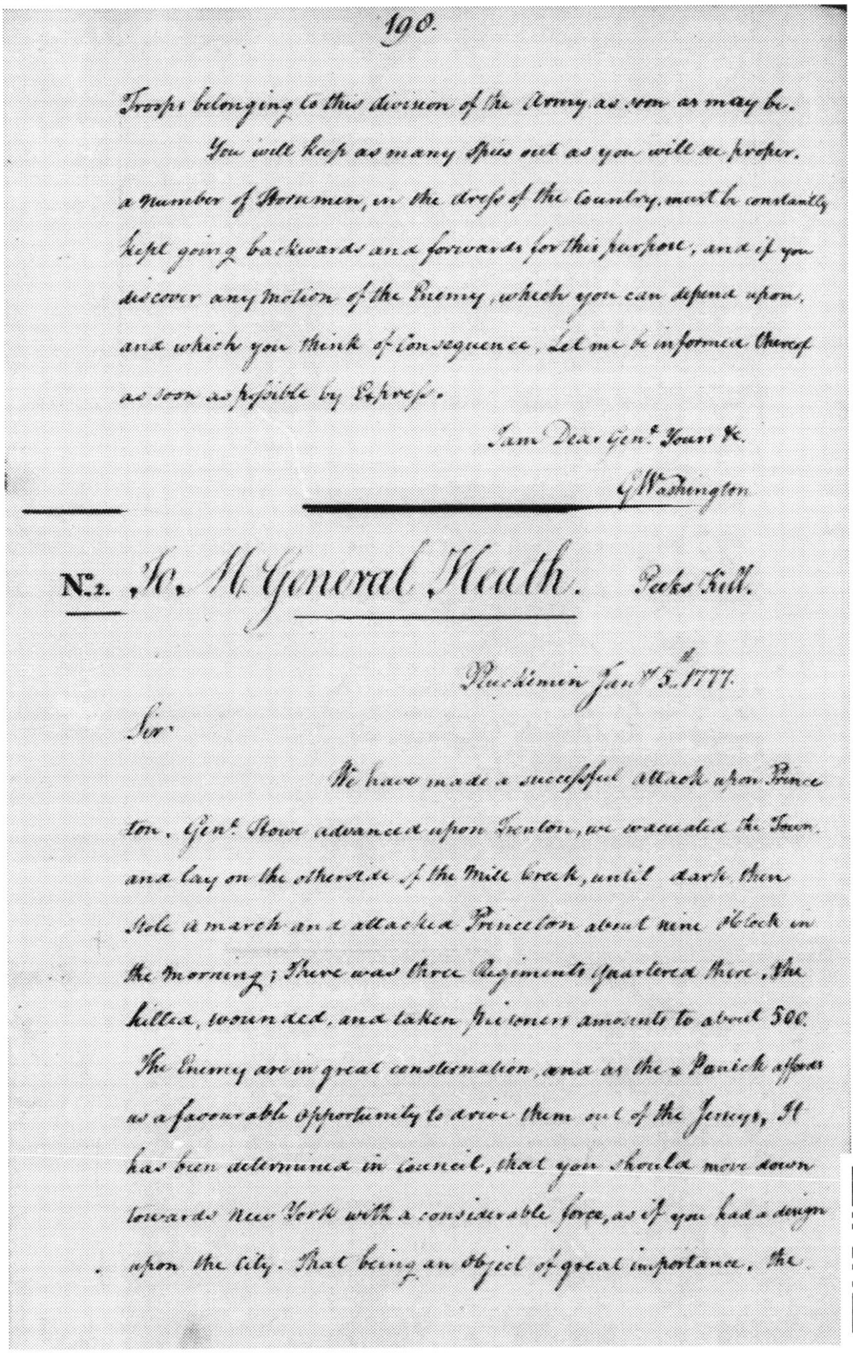

190

Troops belonging to this division of the Army as soon as may be.

You will keep as many Spies out as you will see proper. a number of Horsemen, in the dress of the Country, must be constantly kept going backwards and forwards for this purpose; and if you discover any motion of the Enemy, which you can depend upon, and which you think of consequence, Let me be informed thereof as soon as possible by Express.

I am Dear Genl Yours &c.
G Washington

No.2. To M. General Heath. Peaks Kill.

Buckingham Jany 5th 1777.

Sir

We have made a successful attack upon Princeton. Genl Howe advanced upon Trenton, we evacuated the Town, and lay on the other side of the Mill creek, until dark then stole a march and attacked Princeton about nine oClock in the morning; There was three Regiments quartered there, the killed, wounded, and taken prisoners amounts to about 500. The Enemy are in great consternation, and as the x Panick affords us a favourable opportunity to drive them out of the Jerseys, It has been determined in council, that you should move down towards New York with a considerable force, as if you had a design upon the City. That being an object of great importance, the

The George Washington Papers at the Library of Congress, 1741–1799. Available at www.loc.gov/resource/mgw3b.002/?sp=198. Transcription available at founders.archives.gov/documents/Washington/03-07-02-0412°

Washington Papers at the Library of Congress, 1741–1799 (www.loc.gov/col-lections/george-washington-papers^q) and the National Archives and Records Administration's *Founders Online* website (founders.archives.gov), using key words of Washington and/or Cadwalader and dates of December 1776 and January 1777.

Several accounts constructed by participants at the Battle of Princeton were published years later and can provide additional insight. Two such examples include:

- Sergeant R_____, "The Battle of Princeton," *The Pennsylvania Magazine of History and Biography* 20, no. 4 (1896): 515–519, and
- Thomas Sullivan, "The Battle of Princeton," *The Pennsylvania Magazine of History and Biography* 32, no. 1 (1908): 54–57.

Much can be learned from these primary sources that can help corroborate and/or refute the student's constructed argument, but additional information can be gleaned from websites mentioned earlier, as well as other sites such as the Clarke House Volunteers' *Visit Princeton Battlefield* (www.visitprinceton battlefield.org/visit-princeton-battlefield/ten-crucial-days/battle-of-princeton^r). Additionally, children's books such as Elaine Landau's *George Washington Crosses the Delaware: Would You Risk the Revolution?* (2009) and Margery Cuyler's *The Battlefield Ghost* (2011) are valuable resources for students when constructing better conceptual understandings and narratives about the past. Last, teachers can provide historians' accounts so that students can read powerful commentary from experts, such as the thought that "Howe and Cornwallis had been completely outgeneraled, outwitted, outfought" and that the major impact from this battle was to show the world that "British regulars could be routed, shattered, and captured in large numbers" (Wertenbaker, 1922).

ESTABLISHING A PLAUSIBLE NARRATIVE

During the sixth stage (*Establish a Plausible Narrative*), students take the information gathered during the first five stages to construct a plausible narrative, based on the available evidence, to answer the essential question, "In your estimation, to what extent was the campaign on Princeton a prudent and successful one?" This can be done in numerous ways. In addition to traditional text-based narratives, students can construct websites, documentary videos, computer-based presentations, dioramas, or other creations to demonstrate the understandings that they have developed throughout the previous stages and to adequately address the essential guiding question. I like the option of creating a documentary, a historical marker, or an article for a history magazine, as in each option, students can utilize the sources analyzed and used throughout the investigation to provide an evidence-based argument that can easily be assessed by the teacher to ascertain the level of student understanding.

SUMMARIZING FINAL THOUGHTS

In the final stage (*Summarize Final Thoughts*), students are asked to revisit the investigation they conducted throughout the SOURCES process and metacognitively analyze what was learned, how the knowledge was acquired, how differences in opinion present in the sources were handled, and what questions were left unanswered. They should discuss this with classmates and, if time permits, determine a plan for approaching historical investigation with primary sources in the future and specifically how to attend to lingering questions particular to this exploration. Although additional questions and thoughts may persist, students should have been able to go through the stages of thinking historically and been able to provide an evidence-based narrative to answer the essential question posed at the beginning of the investigation.

CONCLUSION

Through the investigation of a variety of sources and by using the SOURCES framework to scaffold the inquiry process, students can construct their own evidence-based argumentative narrative to respond to the essential question: "In your estimation, to what extent was the campaign on Princeton a prudent and successful one?" Students can debate the prudence and success of this campaign. Most will come to an understanding that there were many different factors and elements facing General Washington in early January 1777, and crucial decisions that impacted the outcome of the revolution had to be made in a limited period of time. Regardless, the evidence will show that the Princeton campaign was a resounding success and was probably the most prudent decision that could have been made at that time, considering the confounding factors that were present.

After this investigation, some students may wonder what happened next and want to learn about whether Washington continued on to New Brunswick. Additional sources can show that Washington gave up the plan of continuing on to New Brunswick, as he felt that with the "harassed state of our troops (many of them having no rest for two nights and a day), and the danger of losing the advantage we had gained by aiming at too much, induced me, by the advice of my officers, to relinquish the attempt" (Washington, 1777). Students can learn that Washington and the Continental Army ended the day in Millstone, continued on to Pluckemin, and on the fifth day arrived at Morristown, where they spent the winter. Unfortunately, the British stores and munitions taken at Princeton were minimal, including the acquisition of blankets, shoes, and a few other items. Although the Continental Army did not cause significant damage to the British, the victories at Trenton and Princeton did force Howe to rethink his tactics and, more importantly, increased morale and public opinion (Ellis, 2004). Henry Knox noted that if they had had 1,000 additional fresh men, they could have moved on to New Brunswick and "struck one of the most brilliant strokes in all history" (Knox, 1777).

QR CODES FOR LINKS IN TEXT

CHAPTER 4

Building Capacity for Student Agency

Using Baseball-Related Primary Sources and the SOURCES Framework

Because many students have interest in and knowledge about sports, one way to demonstrate the capacity for individuals and groups to impact their community and serve as change agents is through the investigation of America's pastime of baseball. Through a variety of sources from different periods of time in American history and with the use of the SOURCES Framework for Teaching With Primary and Secondary Sources, students are able to authentically think about the essential question "How have Americans used sports as a tool for agency or civic engagement?" To pique interest, students can begin by looking at the poem entitled "Base-Ball" (www.loc.gov/resource/rbc0001. 2003juv05880/?sp=51; Figure 4.1). This poem is found in the book *A Little Pretty Pocket-Book*, first published in England in 1744 about outdoor activities suitable to "instruct and amuse" children. The first American edition was published in Worcester, Massachusetts, in 1787. Although legend has it that Abner Doubleday invented the sport in 1839, this source, as well as many others, helps to debunk that myth. By investigating various sources, the teacher can also discuss with students the evolution of the name of the game itself, from Base-Ball (1787), to base-ball (1799), to base ball (1818), to Base Ball (1845), and eventually to baseball (1899).

Figure 4.1. "Base-Ball"—From *A Little Pretty Pocket-Book*

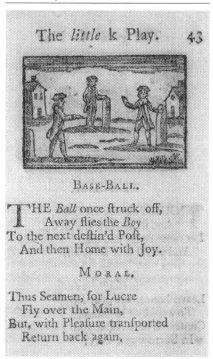

SCRUTINIZING THE FUNDAMENTAL SOURCE(S)

Once students have thought about the game of baseball, the teacher can inquire as to how a sport such as baseball can be used as a tool for civic engagement. The essential question to be posed for this investigation then can be something like "How have Americans used sports as a tool for agency or civic engagement?" In a source from 1916, "Girls Organize Sure 'Nough Ball Club—Know How to Play" (chroniclingamerica.loc.gov/lccn/sn83045487/1916-01-06/ed-1/seq-5; Figure 4.2), students can learn how Ida Schnall felt the need for

GIRLS ORGANIZE SURE 'NOUGH BALL CLUB— KNOW HOW TO PLAY

Figure 4.2. Girls Organize Sure 'Nough Ball Club—Know How to Play—From *The Day Book*

Ida Schnall, Captain of the Feminine Baseball Club at Los Angeles.

A feminine baseball club composed of girls who really understand the game has been organized by motion picture actresses at Los Angeles.

Daily tryouts for places on the team are being held, suits and equipment have been ordered and a schedule of games with similar organizations throughout the state is being made.

Miss Ida Schnall, as captain and manager, has her hands full attending to the various details of the new club and looking over the fair recruits, who are besieging the diamond in an attempt to land on the team. She was formerly captain of the New York Female Giants.

Miss Schnall, who is an expert swimmer and diver, came west from the creation of a female baseball team in Los Angeles, especially after seeing the success of the New York Female Giants and given the absence of any teams on the West Coast of the United States. She decided to replicate in her home of Los Angeles what she had seen in New York. Students should be reminded that this is during a time when women were denied the right to vote, so many may have been discouraged when thinking about the prospect of creating an all-women's baseball team. When examining this newspaper article through the assistance of the use of the SOURCES Analysis Sheet (Figure 1.12), students can learn that more than 20 players showed up for the first tryout and the numbers increased daily. This was considered a testament to the interest in an all-women's team, and it was ultimately a good problem to have, as Schnall's "greatest difficulty now seems to be the final choice of first team players." Students can conclude that there was an apparent interest in having a female team in the Los Angeles area, and, thanks to Ida, this became a reality.

ORGANIZING THOUGHTS

After examining the fundamental source and having a better understanding of what the source is, students need to consider what they know about the geographic, political, social, and historical context in which the source is located, what they know about the source, what they think they know, what they wonder about the source, and what they do not know. To help them in engaging with this source and putting it into context, students should be asked to think about any extracurricular activities in which they are involved. Those who play sports and musical instruments, are scouts, have been members of academic clubs, and/or have participated in other organizations should be asked to think critically about how they became members, how they think those groups came to be, and what would change if the groups had not existed. All students should be asked to think about what clubs or groups they wish existed. Then they should think about the steps necessary for the creation of these sorts of groups or organizations and how the level of difficulty in creating them today would differ from the level at various points in time in American history, especially during the second decade of the 20th century.

UNDERSTANDING THE CONTEXT

Depending on the age of the students, it may be difficult for them to truly grasp the complexity of advocating for and creating a women's baseball team in 1916. To help students gain a better understanding, further contextual information can be discussed. Students should be instructed that this team came together when women were denied the right to vote and that the 19th

Amendment to the Constitution of the United States was not passed by Congress until June 4, 1919. They can also be informed that in 1916, a dozen eggs cost 38¢, a gallon of milk delivered to one's home cost 36¢, and a pound of coffee cost 30¢ (United States Bureau of the Census, 1975). Thus, it was a very different time, and societal norms and standards were quite different then from today.

To further bolster their knowledge, various selections from children's literature can be shared with the students. In *Bloomer Girls: Women Baseball Pioneers (Sport and Society)*, Debra A. Shattuck uses various primary sources to document the history of women's organized baseball clubs and tells how the women involved were treated with condescension, faced countless obstacles, became agents of the women's rights movement, and transformed society's perceptions of women's physical and mental capacity. Other books, like *No Girls in the Clubhouse: The Exclusion of Women from Baseball* by Marilyn Cohen and the *Encyclopedia of Women and Baseball* by Leslie A. Heaphy, can help create a better understanding of the struggles in the creation of female baseball teams and leagues. Students may also be interested in the All-American Girls Professional Baseball League, which was founded and first hosted games in 1943. Films like *A League of Their Own*, and books such as *Players in Pigtails* by Shana Corey and *Mama Played Baseball* by David A. Adler, provide students with more information and context related to this league. Students could also learn about the creation of the Girl Scouts in 1912 by reading *Here Come the Girl Scouts! The Amazing All-True Story of Juliette "Daisy" Gordon Low and Her Great Adventure* by Shana Corey. Books about the women's suffrage movement, such as *Bold & Brave: Ten Heroes Who Won Women the Right to Vote* by Kirsten Gillibrand and *Miss Paul and the President: The Creative Campaign for Women's Right to Vote* by Dean Robbins, can allow students to gain a better understanding of the struggles facing women in the early 20th century.

READING BETWEEN THE LINES

With a better understanding of the time period, of obstacles facing women in the early 20th century, and of how one might go about constructing women's teams and organizations at that time, students should revisit the fundamental source (Girls Organize Sure 'Nough Ball Club—Know How to Play) and think about how their understanding of this source has changed, especially in the context of the essential question, "How have Americans used sports as a tool for agency or civic engagement?" They can be asked to focus on the line "Miss Ida Schnall, as captain and manager, has her hands full attending to the various details of the new club" and what this might mean, especially considering the obstacles and resistance that the creation of a female baseball club might encounter. Once they have considered this, placed the sources within the proper context, and have a better understanding of the content, the students are ready to construct a tentative mental narrative and to move to the *Corroborating and Refuting* stage.

CORROBORATING AND REFUTING

Around the same time as the creation of the female baseball team in Los Angeles, there were increased efforts to make the lives of America's youth better, such as greater focus on various health-related issues and conditions, increased educational opportunities, and limitations on child labor. With this in mind, students can examine and discuss a source published in 1914 entitled "Playground baseball league takes boys off streets and puts them into health" (chronic lingamerica.loc.gov/lccn/sn83045487/1914-02-26/ed-1/seq-27; Figure 4.3). From this source, one can learn that Radowe Abeken, "the young and enthusiastic head of the playgrounds in St. Louis has started a vigorous campaign to organize every playground system of the large cites of the Unites States into one great league of municipal amateur baseball teams" so that collectively they may be able to "keep many boys away from the street corner gangs."

This can provide an opportunity to discuss ways in which individuals have utilized sports to improve conditions and lives throughout history and then transition into how this is being done today and how one might use sports to help others. Students should be reminded of the essential question for this investigation, "How have Americans used sports as a tool for agency or civic engagement?," and should be encouraged to think of how to respond to this question beyond just the efforts made in the past or of ways this is true in a more contemporary context. This way, students can think about how Americans, as well as people across the globe, continue to use sports as a tool for agency and civic engagement.

Conversations also can be had about how baseball was used during wartime. In the image *Union Prisoners at Salisbury, N.C.* (www.loc.gov/pictures/item/94508290; Figure 4.4), students can view how the American Civil War added to the popularity of baseball. Union officers encouraged off-duty soldiers to play the game in order to increase morale and foster camaraderie; additionally, Union prisoners held in Confederate camps taught Southerners about the game and played baseball games within the camps.

As baseball gained popularity through the second half of the 19th century, Japanese Americans began to see baseball as "a critical force in shaping identity, binding ethnic enclaves, forging ties with Japanese culture and promoting civil rights" (Maloney, 2018). Because baseball leagues in the United States were not integrated, Japanese Americans were prohibited from playing in organized leagues, so many looked to create their own leagues. The first team fielding Japanese Americans arose in San Francisco in 1903, with the

Figure 4.3. Playground Baseball League Takes Boys Off Streets and Puts Them Into Health

By Hugh S. Fullerton.

St. Louis may the joke of major league baseball, but that city has advanced and developed an idea which, if extended to every city and town in America, would be the greatest possible development of our national game, and one of the greatest things for the youth of American cities ever planned.

The Playground Baseball League of St. Louis has proved such a success that several other cities are taking up the plan. Cincinnati, Cleveland and Pittsburgh authorities have studied it.

Radowe Abeken, the young and enthusiastic head of the playgrounds in St. Louis, has started a vigorous campaign to organize every playground system of the large cities of the United States into one great league of municipal amateur baseball teams, directly controlled by the playground officials of the cities. At the recent meeting of the National Association of Amateur Baseball Clubs, held in Chicago, Abeken appealed to the promoters to indorse his municipal league and have the amateur teams from the playgrounds of different cities meet each fall for a national championship.

The St. Louis plan is the first comprehensive one put into effect, although many of the other cities have their playground teams. Abeken, when he left college, went into the playground work with the idea that the greatest success could be attained through devoting the most attention to the game most popular among the boys. He threw open the playgrounds of St. Louis to all the boy teams of the city.

At the start little effort was made to control the teams save to allot to them the playing hours. In this way the boys came to look upon the playground authorities as the proper ones to decide disputes, and they became the real government of amateur baseball in St. Louis.

Within a short time even outside teams appealed to the playground authorities for decisions. The move

Figure 4.4. Union Prisoners at Salisbury, NC

Available at www.loc.gov/item/94508290/)

creation of the Fuji Athletic Club. As leagues and teams consisting of Japanese Americans continued to develop and evolve, first-generation immigrants began to see baseball as a modern equivalent of Kendo or Judo, with many seeing it as a sport that illustrated their dedication to American ideals and presented an opportunity to keep children away from "boozing, drugging or gambling their lives away in American environs" (blogs.loc.gov/loc/2018/05/japanese-americas-pastime-baseball[a]). After the bombing of Pearl Harbor and the introduction of internment camps for those of Japanese ancestry, many of the internees turned to baseball to preserve some semblance of a normal life and provide a distraction from the life within the camps. In a photograph included in the *Manzanar Free Press* newspaper (Manzanar, California), from July 27, 1942, students can see an image of baseball being played in Manzanar with a caption that reads, "Baseball . . . Manzanar's favorite sport. One of 180 teams in action" (www.loc.gov/item/sn84025948/1942-07-27/ed-1; Figure 4.5). This is just one example out of many of Japanese American internees using baseball to raise dipping morale in Japanese internment camps. To take this investigation a step further, the teacher can read *Baseball Saved Us*, by Ken Mochizuki, and utilize various sources found on the Library of Congress

Figure 4.5. Photograph by Ansel Adams from 1943 entitled "Baseball game, Manzanar Relocation Center, Calif."

website, as well as those in the Japanese Internment Camp primary source set (www.loc.gov/teachers/classroommaterials/primarysourcesets/internment[b]).

Another source that builds understanding and allows for corroboration and refuting outlines the creation of the All-American Girls Professional Baseball League in 1943. Due to the fact that many young men were being drafted into the service, professional baseball teams were having difficulty fielding teams, and baseball stadium owners were fearful of what might happen with an absence of baseball (All-American Girls Professional Baseball League, n.d.). Phillip J. Wrigley, the owner of the Chicago Cubs, introduced the idea of the creation of a women's softball league that could utilize the now-empty stadiums. During the existence of the league from 1943 to 1954, more than 600 women had the opportunity to play professional baseball. To allow students to understand the importance of this league to the women who played it, the theme song co-written by players Pepper Paire and Nalda Bird can be examined:

Victory Song

Batter up! Hear that call!
The time has come for one and all
To play ball.

We are the members of the All-American League
We come from cities near and far

We've got Canadians, Irishmen, and Swedes,
We're all for one, we're one for all
We're all Americans!!

Each girl stands, her head so proudly high,
Her motto "Do or Die"
She's not the one to use or need an alibi.

Our chaperones are not too soft,
They're not too tough,
Our managers are on the ball.
We've got a president who really knows his stuff,
We're all for one, we're one for all,
We're All-Americans!

Portions of the fictionalized feature film about this baseball league, *A League of Their Own*, such as the scene when the players sing the league theme song, can be shared to increase understanding and empathy. Additionally, students may enjoy reading *The Rules of Conduct* (chicagology.com/baseball/allamericangirlsbaseballleague[c]) and learning that uniforms, hairstyles, and even how members conducted themselves when not playing was regulated. The players faced a fine of $5 for a first offense, $10 for a second, and would be suspended for a third infraction of the league rules. Additional sources may be utilized, but those presented here should allow each of the students an opportunity to establish an evidence-based narrative in response to the essential question posed at the beginning of the investigation.

ESTABLISHING A PLAUSIBLE NARRATIVE

There are many ways in which students could go about demonstrating knowledge and understanding of "How have Americans used sports as a tool for agency or civic engagement?" The creation of a website documenting their thoughts in response to the essential question is one good option. A website can be quite a powerful way for them to demonstrate their understanding and show how they formulated an evidence-based response to wrap up the investigation. This can be enjoyable for the students, can easily be shared with family and friends, and can allow a way for the students to quickly link to and utilize sources beyond those used in class. Further examples and ideas of Web 2.0 tools will be presented in Chapter 10 of this book, and I will demonstrate ways that students can harness the power of the Internet by using images, audio, video, and more in the creation of plausible narratives and share them with various Web 2.0 applications.

SUMMARIZING FINAL THOUGHTS

In the final stage of the framework, students need to examine their thoughts regarding the investigation, but teachers should also engage with them and prompt further considerations. By tying this all to the present and to more contemporary issues, teachers may help to empower students to become change agents themselves. Teachers can provide more contemporary examples of children becoming civically engaged through various types of sports. Instances of current youth involvement and activism, such as efforts for heads-up tackling in football, erasing racism through soccer and other sports, combating racial violence, and the creation of community teams and leagues in underprivileged areas can all be discussed in the classroom. This may lead to opportunities for the students to become more actively involved in sports or other youth programs in their communities and to gain a better appreciation of the ability of athletes to enable change.

CONCLUSION

By using primary sources in the classroom, students are able to examine multiple perspectives to enrich their critical-thinking and problem-solving skills. Rather than telling students what they can do, teachers can allow them the freedom to examine and discuss what others have done to bring about change; this empowers them and encourages civic engagement, whether individually or through community collaborations. Using primary sources when teaching civic ideals and instilling civic-mindedness can go way beyond a simple discussion of our nation's founding documents, as teachers can find a variety of primary sources related to the interests of their students, such as sports, to effectively accomplish this. Utilizing the SOURCES framework gives students the skills and ability to interact with and analyze sources from the past, and even those of today—skills that will help them more effectively examine and question sources they encounter on a daily basis. The ultimate goal of examining sources in this manner is to help students realize and believe that citizenship is not a spectator sport and that, without action, change is not possible.

QR CODES FOR LINKS IN TEXT

a.   b.   c.

CHAPTER 5

What Motivated the Wright Brothers?

An Application of the SOURCES Framework

Although the Wright Brothers are often credited with being the first in flight, as Orville Wright is considered the first person to successfully accomplish a sustained flight in a heavier-than-air mechanically powered plane, some wish to debate as to whether Glenn H. Curtiss, Clément Ader, Gustave Whitehead, Alberto Santos-Dumont, or other candidates for this honor should receive the credit. Despite this, it is a fact that on December 17, 1902, at Kitty Hawk, North Carolina, the plane, known as the Wright Flyer and piloted by Orville Wright, flew over a distance of 120 feet and remained aloft for more than 12 seconds. Through the analysis of primary sources, one can learn a tremendous amount about the Wright Brothers; their plans; the design, construction, fabric, propulsion system, and flight controls of the Flyer; and details about the trials and successes of Orville and Wilbur Wright (see the online exhibit, The Wright Brothers & The Invention of the Aerial Age, at airandspace.si.edu/exhibitions/wright-brothers-invention-aerial-age[a]). Despite the debate that exists, one thing for sure is that the Wright brothers were interested in mechanical flight, and one inquiry that can capture students' interest is to try to determine where this desire to fly originated, how serious it was, and through what means it was facilitated. As the topic of first flight, how people impacted history, and the rapid acceleration of innovations from the time of the Wright Brothers' first flight are typical topics covered in various classrooms, the SOURCES Framework for Teaching With Primary and Secondary Sources (Figure 1.13) is an excellent scaffold to facilitate the exploration of the Wright Brothers' motivation.

SCRUTINIZING THE FUNDAMENTAL SOURCE(S)

Even though one could easily begin an inquiry investigation about the Wright Brothers with questions focusing on their early life or their collaboration as printers (*West Side News*), bicycle-shop founders (Wright Cycle Company), or inventors, this SOURCES investigation begins on May 30, 1899, with a letter written by Wilbur to the Smithsonian Institution (airandspace.

**Figure 5.1. Letter
from Wilbur Wright
Dated May 30, 1899**

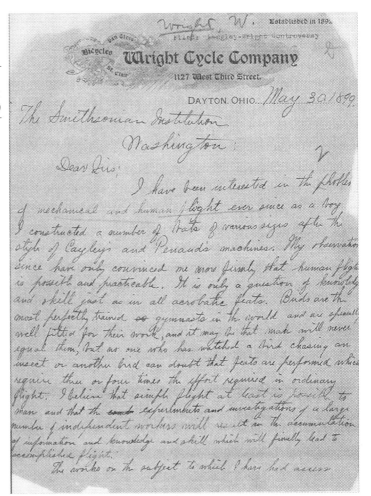

si.edu/collection-objects/wright-wilbur-wright-brothers-correspondence-
si-1899-photograph; Figure 5.1). It is thought to be the first documented evidence pointing toward the Wright brothers' serious interest in the possibility
of mechanical and human flight.

As students analyze the letter using the SOURCES Analysis Sheet (Figure
1.12), they should think about the essential questions for this SOURCES-
based exploration, "What motivated the Wright Brothers? Was it passion, just
a way to pass the time, and/or simply a paycheck?" In this letter, which is
one of two fundamental sources used in this investigation, Wilbur writes that
he has been "interested in the problem of mechanical and human flight ever
since as a boy I constructed a number of bats of various sizes," and he has
determined that his "observations since have only convinced me more firmly
that human flight is possible and practicable." Analysis of the letter allows

the readers to gain insight into his thinking and what has led him to pursue human flight. He states that flight is "only a question of knowledge and skill just as in all acrobatic feats." He discusses observations he has made of birds and that he is going to begin a "systematic study of the subject in preparation for practical work to which I expect to devote what time I can spare from my regular business." At this time, he also contacts the Smithsonian as he wishes to obtain papers and any writings that they have focusing on studies, theories, and thoughts regarding flights. He concludes the letter by offering his services to fellow researchers and providing assurance to the recipient that he is "an enthusiast, but not a crank in the sense that I have some pet theories as to the proper construction of a flying machine."

The letter written by Wilbur Wright on May 30, 1899, can be followed with a second fundamental source, which is another letter from Wilbur, dated May 13, 1900 (www.loc.gov/item/wright002804; Figure 5.2). This letter is written to aviation pioneer Octave Chanute, who is living in Chicago, Illinois, at the time. The choice of words that Wilbur uses even in the introduction is powerful, as one can get a sense of his passion for flight. He writes:

> For some years I have been afflicted with the belief that flight is possible to man. My disease has increased in severity and I feel that it will soon cost me an increased amount of money if not my life.

He argues to Mr. Chanute that it is "possible to fly without motors, but not without knowledge & skill," which is "fortunate, for man, by reason of his greater intellect, can more reasonably hope to equal birds in knowledge, than to equal nature in the perfection of her machinery." The main purpose of the letter is for Wilbur to detail:

> the plan and apparatus it is my intention to test. In explaining these, my object is to learn to what extent similar plans have been tested and found to be failures and also to obtain such suggestions as your great knowledge and experience might enable you to give me.

As one considers his true intentions, it can be read that Wilbur believes that:

> no financial profit will accrue to the inventor of the first flying machine, and that only those who are willing to give as well as to receive suggestions can hope to link their names with the honor of its discovery. The problem is too great for one man alone and unaided to solve in secret.

Wilbur goes on to explain in clear detail his plans for achieving flight. He notes his observations of buzzards, his knowledge of previous attempts, including Mr. Chanute's efforts in 1896–1897, and how his plan differs from others:

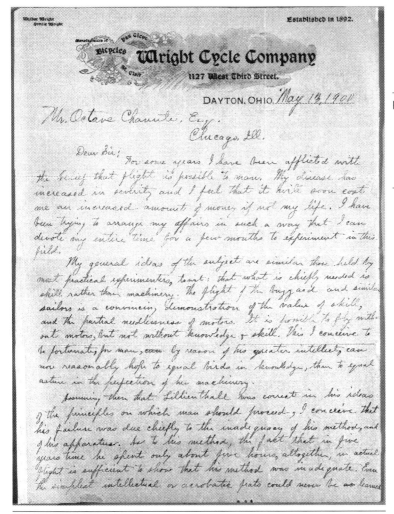

(Transcript available at invention.psychology.msstate.edu/i/Wrights/library
/Chanute_Wright_correspond/May13-1900.html[b]).

Figure 5.2. Octave
Chanute
Papers: Special
Correspondence—
Wright Brothers,
1900

cross-stays which prevent the upper plane from moving forward and backward
are removed, and each end of the upper plane is independently moved forward
or backward with respect to the lower plane by a suitable lever or other arrange-
ment. By this plan the whole upper plane may be moved forward or backward,
to attain longitudinal equilibrium, by moving both hands forward or backward
together. Lateral equilibrium is gained by moving one end more than the other or
by moving them in opposite directions. . . . My plan is to attach the tail rigidly to
the rear upright stays which connect the planes, the effect of which will be that
when the upper plane is thrown forward the end of the tail is elevated, so that the
tail assists gravity in restoring longitudinal balance.

Wilber also notes that he "would be particularly thankful for advice as to a suitable locality where I could depend on winds of about fifteen miles per hour without rain or too inclement weather. I am certain that such localities are rare." It is interesting to read in Octave Chanute's response on May 17, 1900, that several locations may be suitable but that he believes that "better locations can be found on the Atlantic coasts of South Carolina or Georgia." After careful examination of the fundamental sources and consideration of conceptual understandings, it is time for students to organize their thoughts as they pursue an evidence-based argument for the essential question, "What motivated the Wright Brothers? Was it passion, just a way to pass the time, and/or simply a paycheck?"

ORGANIZING THOUGHTS

During the *Organize Thoughts* stage, students should think about what they knew prior to reading the letters authored by Wilbur Wright. They can work individually or in small groups, but it may be most beneficial at this point if the teacher leads them in a class discussion about what they know, how the letter added to or modified their understanding, and what else they would like to know. Students can be given several minutes to Think, Pair, and Share their thinking in small groups of two or three and to develop questions to guide the remainder of the lesson, while focusing on the essential question posed for the investigation. A perfect scaffold to utilize here and have the student complete in small groups is the SOURCES Analysis Sheet (Figure 1.12).

UNDERSTANDING THE CONTEXT

There are many resources available to assist students in building their content knowledge and to help them to better *Understand the Context*. The context is vital to understanding the time period in which the source is situated and the sources to be examined. Such knowledge empowers the students to properly attend to the essential question, "What motivated the Wright Brothers? Was it passion, just a way to pass the time, and/or simply a paycheck?" The following are excellent books for helping students to put this investigation into proper context and to learn more about the thoughts, intentions, and lives of Orville and Wilbur Wright:

Borden, L., & Marx, T. (2003). *Touching the sky: The flying adventures of Wilbur and Orville Wright*. New York, NY: Margaret K. McElderry Books.
Buckley, J. (2014). *Who were the Wright Brothers?* New York, NY: Grosset and Dunlap.
Busby, P. (2002). *First to fly: How Wilbur and Orville Wright invented the airplane*. New York, NY: Crown Publishers.

Collins, M. (2003). *Airborne: A photobiography of Wilbur and Orville Wright*. Washington, DC: National Geographic.

Freedman, R. (1991). *The Wright Brothers: How they invented the airplane*. New York, NY: Holiday House.

Glass, A. (2003). *The wondrous whirligig: The Wright Brothers' first flying machine*. New York, NY: Holiday House.

Gutman, D. (2003). *Race for the sky: The Kitty Hawk diaries of Johnny Moore*. New York, NY: Simon and Schuster.

READING BETWEEN THE LINES

At this stage of the inquiry process, provide students with copies of the two fundamental sources that started the investigation, the two letters written by Wilbur Wright (May 30, 1899 and May 13, 1900). Encourage students to think about how they interpreted what they read in these letters initially and how their understanding has changed. They should think about what has changed and what it was that made them modify their understanding of the possible motivations of Orville and Wilbur Wright to pursue flight at Kitty Hawk and beyond.

CORROBORATING AND REFUTING

As students develop their understanding of what truly motivated the Wright brothers and what their intentions were as they pursued mechanical flight, they should be given an opportunity to begin developing a narrative in response to the essential question guiding the investigation, "What motivated the Wright Brothers? Was it passion, just a way to pass the time, and/or simply a paycheck?," as well as any additional questions of their own. Each of the following sources are used as they refer to the motivations of the Wright brothers. Thus, each source helps students build an appropriate, evidence-based response:

- Orville Wright letter to his father on September 3, 1900
  - » www.loc.gov/resource/mwright.02055/?sp=4[c]
  - » Letter where he notes that flight is possible and that he is doing his experiments for pleasure, not profit.
- Orville Wright's diary entry, December 17, 1903
  - » www.libraries.wright.edu/special/wrightbrothers/educational/orville[d]
  - » Diary entry where he notes how he felt when he made the first flight.

- Wright Brothers' patent for the 1903 Flyer
  - » www.libraries.wright.edu/special/wrightbrothers/patents[c]
  - » This patent was granted to the Wrights in 1906 and protected them from other inventors who might have tried to steal their ideas.
- "The Wright Brother's Aëroplane" by Orville and Wilbur Wright
  - » invention.psychology.msstate.edu/inventors/i/Wrights/library/Century.html[f]
  - » Orville and Wilbur wrote this article, which appeared in the September 1908 issue of *Century Magazine,* to give people a first-person account of how they invented flight.
- "Girls Flew Too"
  - » www.libraries.wright.edu/special/wrightbrothers/educational/girls[g]
  - » A reminiscence by Ivonette Wright Miller, niece of the Wright brothers. Ivonette Wright Miller was one of the first girls to fly in the United States. In this source she remembers what it was like to fly with her Uncle Orville in 1911.

If the teacher wants to include more open inquiry for the students, some of these sites are useful:

- Smithsonian Archives (siarchives.si.edu/history/featured-topics/stories/wright-brothers-pioneers-aviation[h])
- Wright State University Libraries (www.libraries.wright.edu/special/wrightbrothers[i])
- Primary Source Nexus (primarysourcenexus.org/2012/12/today-in-history-wright-brothers-first-flight[j])
- National Parks Service (www.nps.gov/wrbr/learn/historyculture/theroadtothefirstflight.htm[k])
- Smithsonian Institution Classroom Activities (airandspace.si.edu/exhibitions/wright-brothers/online/classroomActivities/8-12_step1.cfm[l])
- Air and Space Magazine (www.airspacemag.com/as-interview/david-mccullough-wright-brothers-180955344[m])

ESTABLISHING A PLAUSIBLE NARRATIVE

In this second-to-last stage of the SOURCES framework, students are expected to create their own original, evidence-based narrative responding to the essential question posed at the beginning of the investigation, "What motivated the Wright Brothers? Was it passion, just a way to pass the time, and/or simply a paycheck?" Throughout the stages of the framework, students should consider whether their major motivator was primarily a passion for flight, maybe just a way to pass the time or earn a paycheck, or any number of other reasons for why they pursued this endeavor. There are many ways to assess student knowledge about the Wright Brothers and their motivations, but I suggest assigning the students a construction project: a historical marker for the Wright brothers' hometown of Dayton, Ohio, or for the site of their flight in Kitty Hawk, North Carolina. They will be expected to provide essential information regarding the brothers' motivations and intentions on the marker, as well as imagery to help convey their understandings.

SUMMARIZING FINAL THOUGHTS

In this last stage, students should *Summarize Final Thoughts*. One way to accomplish this is through small-group discussions, which can help each student to contemplate his or her thoughts about the Wright brothers and their motivations, explore their own feelings about the inquiry process and about how knowledge was acquired, and address any remaining questions. To assist students, the following questions can be posted for their consideration as they reflect upon the entire inquiry process:

- How effective was the inquiry process for you?
- What would you change for next time?
- What content was acquired?
- How was it acquired?
- What questions are left lingering?

CONCLUSION

Through this examination of the motivation of the Wright brothers, students have an opportunity to engage in authentic inquiry-based investigation. They are able to examine original sources, contemplate the essential question, "What motivated the Wright Brothers? Was it passion, just a way to pass the time, and/or simply a paycheck?," and develop evidence-based narratives. Thus, students are given the opportunity to replicate processes and thinking engaged in by experts focusing on science, social sciences, and other disciplines in real-world contexts.

QR CODES FOR LINKS IN TEXT

a.

b.

c.

d.

e.

f.

g.

h.

i.

j.

k.

l.

m.

CHAPTER 6

Using Poetry to Build
the Capacity to Empathize
An Application of the SOURCES Framework

Many different types of sources can help students to learn about other times, people, and places; however, poetry can be extremely powerful, especially when utilizing pieces written by those directly associated with an experience. In the following investigation, students are introduced to a poem entitled "That Damned Fence," and are asked to grapple with the essential question, "As a citizen of the United States in 1942, how justified do you believe the internment of Japanese Americans and those of Japanese ancestry to be?" The students are exposed to a variety of primary sources in an attempt to allow student to empathize with individuals from a different place and time and to take a critical stance on the treatment of Japanese Americans during the Second World War.

SCRUTINIZING THE FUNDAMENTAL SOURCE(S)

For the first stage, *Scrutinizing the Fundamental Source(s)*, of the SOURCES Framework for Teaching With Primary and Secondary Sources, students are given an opportunity to engage with a powerful poem written and shared within a Japanese internment camp during the Second World War. In "That Damned Fence," an anonymous poem that was circulated around the Poston Relocation Center in Yuma County in southwestern Arizona, the author presents the thoughts and emotions felt by many of the Japanese Americans, not only in this camp but across the 10 relocation centers set up by the United States government. I believe that this is a perfect fundamental source to engage students, build empathy, and help them along the inquiry process toward answering the essential question. An example of a family, the Hirano family, interned at Poston Relocation Center can also be shared (https://catalog.archives.gov/id/535989; Figure 6.1), and the feelings and thoughts that they and others might have felt are articulated clearly in the poem "That Damned Fence."

Figure 6.1. The Hirano Family, left to right, George, Hisa, and Yasbei. Colorado River
   Relocation Center, Poston, Arizona.

THAT DAMNED FENCE

They've sunk the posts deep into the ground
They've strung out wires all the way around.
With machine gun nests just over there,
And sentries and soldiers everywhere.

We're trapped like rats in a wired cage,
To fret and fume with impotent rage;
Yonder whispers the lure of the night,
But that DAMNED FENCE assails our sight.

We seek the softness of the midnight air,
But that DAMNED FENCE in the floodlight glare
Awakens unrest in our nocturnal quest,
And mockingly laughs with vicious jest.

With nowhere to go and nothing to do,
We feel terrible, lonesome, and blue:
That DAMNED FENCE is driving us crazy,
Destroying our youth and making us lazy.

Imprisoned in here for a long, long time,
We know we're punished—though we've committed no crime,
Our thoughts are gloomy and enthusiasm damp,
To be locked up in a concentration camp.

Loyalty we know, and patriotism we feel,
To sacrifice our utmost was our ideal,
To fight for our country, and die, perhaps;
But we're here because we happen to be Japs.

We all love life, and our country best,
Our misfortune to be here in the west,
To keep us penned behind that DAMNED FENCE,
Is someone's notion of NATIONAL DEFENCE!

Students should read the poem completely through and think about what it means to them. They should read it over as many times as necessary, and be encouraged to determine what it is that they believe the author is trying to convey, what thoughts may be going through the creator's mind, what this individual and others at Poston and the other camps endured during this time, and in what ways poetry can help people to understand very personal experiences, feelings, and thoughts. To focus their thinking, students should answer specific questions, such as:

- What does the title mean?
- What do you know about the creator?
- What is the topic for the poem?
- When, where, and why was the poem created?
- Do you believe that others created poems like this?
- How might poems created by those interned be similar or how might they differ?

Analysis sheets, such as the SOURCES Analysis Sheet (Figure 1.12) or something more specific to the analysis of poetry like the Poetry Analysis Sheet (www.readwritethink.org/files/resources/lesson_images/lesson1160/poetry _analysis.pdf[a]) provided by the International Literacy Association and the National Council of Teachers of English on their ReadWriteThink website (www.readwritethink.org[b]), can help students to more effectively analyze poetry. Scaffolding, such as this analysis sheet, is quite important to provide, especially since many students have had little to no experience with critically engaging with poetry, thinking about a creator's intentions, or fully appreciating poetry and the messages it conveys, as well as what can be learned from other forms of art.

ORGANIZING THOUGHTS

In the second stage of the SOURCES framework, students need to think carefully about what they know at this point in time about the internment of Japanese Americans and those of Japanese ancestry. They should also critically think about what the author of the poem, "That Damned Fence," is stating, how this might be similar to what others are experiencing, what bias might exist within this and other sources, and how effectively a poem conveys emotion, thoughts, and experiences. Students should organize their thoughts mentally and then write them on a sheet of paper or in a Word document, or record them in an audio or video clip. This should help them to determine what information they need in order to understand the source more thoroughly, to analyze the poem in its proper geographic and historical context, and to attend to the essential question, "As a citizen of the United States in 1942, how justified do you believe the internment of Japanese Americans and those of Japanese ancestry to be?."

UNDERSTANDING THE CONTEXT

To help students to better understand the time and context in which this poem was written, teachers can share a variety of sources, such as news clips from December 1941 about the December 7, 1941, bombing of Pearl Harbor (www.youtube.com/watch?v=A2kSnlS4xX8) or information related to the "date which will live in infamy" speech (Figure 6.2) delivered by President Franklin D. Roosevelt on December 8th:

- Video of the speech (www.youtube.com/watch?v=NlpYyA3dnVI[c])
- Pop-up video version of the infamy speech that provides additional information and context (www.youtube.com/watch?v=7xd8MpR-5Ko[d])
- Transcript of the speech (www.loc.gov/resource/afc1986022. afc1986022_ms2201/?st=text[e])
- An original draft edited by President Roosevelt (www.archives.gov/ publications/prologue/2001/winter/crafting-day-of-infamy-speech. html[f])

A source that should be shared with students is Executive Order 9066 (www.ourdocuments.gov/doc.php?flash=true&doc=74[g]). This order, signed by President Roosevelt on February 19, 1942, allowed the U.S. military to ban and relocate both foreign-born Japanese immigrants (*issei*—meaning "first generation" of Japanese in the United States) and Japanese who were born American citizens (*nisei*—the second generation of Japanese in America, U.S.

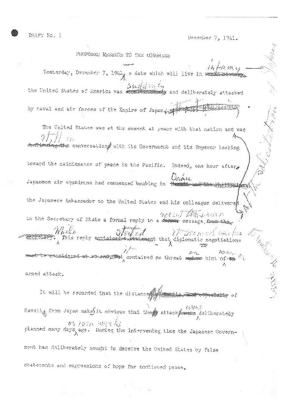

Figure 6.2. President Roosevelt's *Date Which Will Live in Infamy* Draft of Speech

citizens by birthright) from a 50- to 60-mile-wide section of the West Coast of the United States. Additionally, this same order, along with other orders and restrictions, was applied to residents who were of German and Italian descent. Videos created by the U.S. Office of War Information and the War Relocation Authority outlined how what happened at Pearl Harbor was impacting life in the United States; why the relocation and internment of Japanese Americans and those of Japanese ancestry, from its perspective, was necessary; and how the relocation of these individuals would be carried out (archive.org/details/Japanese1943; Figure 6.3).

Another important source to help students gain a better understanding of what was presented to Japanese Americans in the western zone of the United States in 1942, as to what they were to do, bring with them, and how the removal would be conducted, is one of any of the civilian exclusion orders, such as Civilian Exclusion Order #5 (www.loc.gov/resource/cph.3a35053; Figure 6.4). These orders, issued by General John L. DeWitt as the head of the Western Defense Command, were posted in public spaces and included directions for "all persons of Japanese ancestry, including aliens and non-aliens" in this zone as to what they were to do and where they were to go, since it was no longer possible for them to remain on the West Coast of the United States.

Figure 6.3. Screenshot of Film Created by the U.S. Office of War Information and the War Relocation Authority

Figure 6.4. Civilian Exclusion Order #5, Posted at First and Front Streets, Directing Removal by April 7 of Persons of Japanese Ancestry, from the First San Francisco Section to Be Affected by the Evacuation

The language provided in this document is quite direct, can evoke emotion, and helps to remind students of the human aspects associated with this situation (especially #3—No pets of any kind will be permitted). The following is found in one of the orders in regard to those to be interned:

2. Evacuees must carry with them on departure for the Assembly Center, the following property:

    (a) Bedding and linens (no mattress) for each member of the family;
    (b) Toilet articles for each member of the family;
    (c) Extra clothing for each member of the family;
    (d) Sufficient knives, forks, spoons, plates, bowls and cups for each member of the family
    (e) Essential personal effects for each member of the family.

    All items carried will be securely packaged, tied and plainly marked with the name of the owner and numbered in accordance with instructions obtained at the Civil Control Station. The size and number of packages is limited to that which can be carried by the individual or family group.

3. No pets of any kind will be permitted.

4. The United States Government through its agencies will provide for the storage at the sole risk of the owner of the more substantial household items, such as iceboxes, washing machines, pianos and other heavy furniture. Cooking utensils and other small items will be accepted for storage if crated, packed and plainly marked with the name and address of the owner. Only one name and address will be used by a given family.

5. Each family and individual living alone will be furnished transportation to the Assembly Center or will be authorized to travel by private automobile in a supervised group. All instructions pertaining to the movement will be obtained at the Civil Control Station. (lcweb2.loc.gov/service/pnp/cph/3a30000/3a35000/3a35000/3a35053v.jpg[h])

Images of the procedure used during the registering and processing phase, such as one of the evacuation of Japanese Americans at the Santa Anita Reception Center, along with class discussions, will help students to picture how individuals were affected, to think through the impacts upon both children and adults, and to remember that these were American citizens being interned (www.loc.gov/resource/ppmsca.38735; Figure 6.5).

Figure 6.5. The Evacuation of Japanese-Americans From West Coast Areas Under U.S. Army War Emergency Order; Japanese Americans Waiting for Registration at the Santa Anita Reception Center.

Teachers can also share the case of *Korematsu v. United States* (www.oyez. org/cases/1940-1955/323us214[i]) with students. This case involved a Japanese American citizen, Fred Korematsu, who was living in San Leandro, California, at the time when Executive Order 9066 was signed and put into action. He decided that he would not be relocated and remained at his residence, which led to his arrest and conviction for violating the order. Mr. Korematsu argued that Executive Order 9066 violated the Fifth Amendment. The case made it to the United States Supreme Court, and the court ruled 6–3 in favor of the United States, as the majority determined that the executive order did not show racial prejudice. They felt that it necessarily responded to the strategic requirement of keeping the West Coast secure from possible Japanese invasion.

As students engage with these images, videos, and sound recordings, analysis sheets such as the SOURCES Analysis sheet (Figure 1.12) and/or those from the Library of Congress (www.loc.gov/programs/teachers/getting-started -with-primary-sources/guides[j]), the National Archives and Records Administration (www.archives.gov/education/lessons/worksheets[k]) or the SOAPS Primary Source "Think" Sheet (www.teacheroz.com/SOAPPS.pdf[l]), will help students to better understand the content and details within sources and to pick up on various aspects they might otherwise have missed. Any of the sources used in this section could easily be utilized during the *Corroborating and Refuting* stage instead, or as well, if the teacher feels that their student population would benefit from such engagement at that point.

READING BETWEEN THE LINES

Now that deeper contextual understanding is present, students will need to revisit the fundamental source, "That Damned Fence." With added knowledge about the time, place, and people affected, students can now better understand the lines in the poem and the message being conveyed by its creator, such as "we're trapped like rats in a wired cage . . . To fret and fume with impotent rage . . . awakens unrest in our nocturnal quest . . . we know we're punished—though we've committed no crime." These lines would have had little meaning and would not have had the required impact on students if the poem had simply been read without the proper context, and if instruction had convened without additional analysis. Thus, going through these stages allows students to engage with sources in an authentic manner, to better understand the context in which they occur, and to gain empathy for the creator of the source. The framework leads the learner to think about additional questions and how to go about answering the essential question posed at the beginning of the investigation.

CORROBORATING AND REFUTING

As students begin to determine how they will corroborate and refute under-standings developed after engaging with the primary and secondary sources encountered, they need to focus on how to respond to the essential question of "As a citizen of the United States in 1942, how justified do you believe the internment of Japanese Americans and those of Japanese ancestry to be?" Various pieces of children's literature can help them to better respond to the essential question. One such book is *Baseball Saved Us* by Ken Mochizuki. This is a story that describes what was experienced by many Japanese Americans at the time—relocation, life in a camp, ways in which residents coped with their changing life, and how different things were once the war was over. The main character in this book is an adolescent experiencing many of the feelings and pressures typical for children of this age, so this helps students relate to the situation, feelings, and experiences endured. There are many other pow-erful pieces of literature for children and young adults focusing on Japanese internment and relocation that can be used, such as:

- *A Place Where Sunflowers Grow* by Amy Lee-Tai
- *Dear Miss Breed: True Stories of the Japanese American Incarceration During World War II and a Librarian Who Made a Difference* by Joanne Oppenheim
- *Farewell to Manzanar* by Jeanne Wakatsuki Houston
- *Gaijin: American Prisoner of War* by Matt Faulkner
- *Enemy Child: The Story of Norman Mineta, a Boy Imprisoned in a Japanese American Internment Camp During World War II* by Andrea Warren
- *Midnight in Broad Daylight: A Japanese American Family Caught Between Two Worlds* by Pamela Rotner Sakamoto

Being able to view images of the internment camps (www.loc.gov/resource/ppprs.00200; Figure 6.6) and of daily life in the camps (www.loc.gov/resource/ppprs.00368; Figure 6.7) helps students to better empathize with those interned. Additionally, videos of those who were interned talking about their experiences are quite moving and powerful, such as one showing actor George Takei and entitled "Life Inside a Japanese Internment Camp During WWII"_(www.you-tube.com/watch?v=Vpn3k8mxjqY[m]), an interview with actor Pat Morita (www.youtube.com/watch?v=2XpPbBoxBME; Figure 6.8), and a video (Kids Meet a Survivor of the Japanese-American Internment) of an individual who was interned speaking with children about his experiences at that time (www.you-tube.com/watch?v=_e1s2kwSPwU[n]). Many videos about the subject of intern-ment, some featuring those who were interned, can be found on YouTube and on the Internet Archive website (archive.org[o]).

Figure 6.6. Manzanar From Guard Tower, View West (Sierra Nevada in the Background), Manzanar Relocation Center, California

Figure 6.7. Mess Line, Noon, Manzanar Relocation Center, California

Figure 6.8. Screenshot of Video of Pat Morita Discussing His Internment

Students can also freely utilize a variety of online resources to help them respond to the fundamental source. The Library of Congress's website for a primary source set on Japanese American Internment (www.loc.gov/teachers/ classroommaterials/primarysourcesets/internment[p]) offers the user 18 primary sources focusing on the internment experience and a teacher's guide that provides context, teaching suggestions, and links to online resources. Densho (densho.org[q]), named for the Japanese term meaning "to pass on to the next generation," or to leave a legacy, is an organization dedicated to the preservation and dissemination of the history of the World War II incarceration of Japanese Americans with the hope of promoting equity and justice today. The Densho website offers testimonies and images of Japanese Americans who were unjustly incarcerated, as well as teacher resources. A multitude of lesson plans and accompanying sources and resources are available across the Internet from the Library of Congress (www.loc.gov/classroom-materials/japanese-american-internment-fear-itself[r]), the National Archives (www.archives.gov/education /lessons/japanese-relocation/activities.html[s]), the National Endowment for the Humanities (edsitement.neh.gov/lesson-plans/japanese-american-internment-camps-during-wwii[t]), the *New York Times* (www.nytimes.com/2017/12/07/ learning/lesson-plans/teaching-japanese-american-internment-using-primary -resources.html[u]), and the Zinn Education Project (www.zinnedproject.org/ materials/lesson-on-the-japanese-american-internment[v]).

ESTABLISHING A PLAUSIBLE NARRATIVE

Since the fundamental source was a poem, a perfect assessment piece for this investigation would be for the students to construct a poem that allows them to properly attend to the essential question, "As a citizen of the United States in 1942, how justified do you believe the internment of Japanese Americans and those of Japanese ancestry to be?" Many forms of poetry can be utilized, such as an acrostic, haiku, letter, or ballad poem, but a diamante poem can be a powerful way for them to demonstrate that they understand the differing viewpoints at this volatile period in history. Students are asked to create a poem in the shape of a diamond that includes nouns, adjectives, and gerunds to describe one topic or perspective or two diametric viewpoints (e.g., night/day or winter/spring). The Academy of American Poets (poets.org/materials-teachers[w]) and ReadWriteThink (www.readwritethink.org/search/?resource_type=16&type=28[x]) provide useful resources for teachers wanting to include poetry in teaching. Students should be encouraged to share their poetry with others (a poetry reading night could be held at school), and the poems can be shared with parents during an open house event.

SUMMARIZING FINAL THOUGHTS

As students progress through the *Summarizing Final Thoughts* stage, they should be encouraged to think critically about the entire investigation and learning process, specifically focusing on how the use of a poem as the fundamental source helped them to engage with the content. As poetry is rarely utilized for critical-thinking opportunities in the classroom, the hope is that students see poetry as a useful and powerful source and a way to gain a better understanding of the thoughts, experiences, dreams, morals, and character of people just like them or even people from another place and time. Additionally, poetry can be an extremely valuable source when trying to help students understand diverse thoughts and perspectives from various people in contemporary society and to gain a better grasp on current events, conflicts, and controversies.

CONCLUSION

In this investigation, students are asked to empathize with individuals from a very different place and time. The use of a poem as the fundamental source is a powerful way to help students critically analyze the context in which the source is situated, to understand the perspectives of the individuals involved, and, most importantly, to build the capacity to have empathy for others. The essential question, "As a citizen of the United States in 1942, how justified do you believe the internment of Japanese Americans and those of Japanese ancestry to be?," can be a difficult topic to broach. By using the SOURCES framework to scaffold the actual voices and imagery of those who lived through this event and time, students can gain a better understanding of what happened and how the people involved were affected. In turn, they will find ways to use this understanding and this process to think critically about contemporary issues and events.

QR CODES FOR LINKS IN TEXT

CHAPTER 7

Teaching Controversial Literature
An Application of the SOURCES Framework

Teachers often find themselves being required to teach topics and curricula that cause them discomfort, are controversial, or even with which they do not agree. In situations like these, primary and secondary sources can be extremely powerful. One example of this is the use of materials and curriculum related to Mark Twain and his works. While there is controversy in using *The Adventures of Huckleberry Finn* (upload.wikimedia.org/wikipedia/commons/6/6d/E._W._Kemble_-_Adventures_of_Huckleberry_Finn_Cover.jpg; Figure 7.1) in the classroom, many school districts and teachers across the United States continue to utilize this text. Whether a requirement or a personal choice, teaching *Huckleberry Finn* provides an opportunity to carefully analyze the characterization of one of the central figures of the book, Jim, as well as the treatment of African Americans during this period in American history in literature, media, and popular culture. To gain a better understanding of life for African Americans at this time, the reading of *Huckleberry Finn* can be paired with autobiographies by former slaves such as Frederick Douglass (upload.wikimedia.org/wikipedia/commons/8/8b/Frederick_Douglass_as_a_younger_man.jpg; Figure 7.2) and Solomon Northup, to add insight into the lives of these individuals and demonstrate the levels of uniqueness, intelligence, and diversity possessed by people who were far too often dehumanized, as well as learn firsthand about atrocities that were endured by millions of people throughout a large portion of American history. Other powerful and impactful sources that can be used are the ones from the Federal Writers' Project, a funded project in which scholars and students were compensated to travel the southern areas of the United States to interview elderly African Americans who were formerly enslaved and to document their personal narratives.

One often-neglected but useful type of resource that should be used in conjunction with *Huckleberry Finn* or any content related to the enslavement of African Americans is fugitive slave ads. Fugitive, or runaway, slave advertisements were purchased and published in newspapers throughout the United States during the 18th and 19th centuries by slaveowners looking for runaway slaves (blogs.loc.gov/headlinesandheroes/2019/10/runaway-fugitive-slave-ads-in-newspapers; Figure 7.3). Fugitive slave ads can bring much understanding

Figure 7.1.
Adventures of Huckleberry Finn Cover

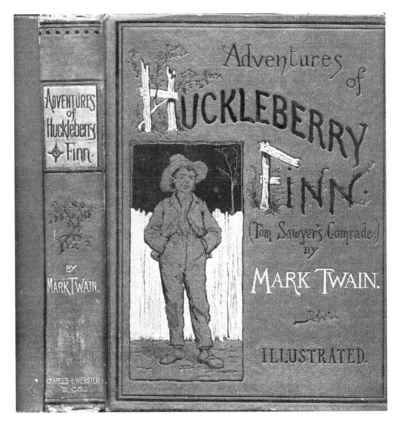

Figure 7.2. Frederick Douglass as a Younger Man

**Figure 7.3. "TWENTY DOLLARS REWARD.
RAN AWAY,"** *Southern Telegraph*
(Rodney, MS), August 9, 1836, p. 6.

TWENTY DOLLARS REWARD.
RAN AWAY from the planta-
tion of the subscriber, lying in
Warren County, ten miles from
Vicksburg, some time in February
last, a Negro Boy, named

PETER,

about 18 or 20 years of age, five feet seven
or eight inches high, well proportioned in
make, very active and sprightly; has a
pleasing countenance, smiles when spoken
to, and is very intelligent; slightly inclined
to the mulatto in color, and has a scar on
his face, but not recollected where. He
took with him several articles of clothing,
amongst which was a coat of Kentucky
janes that reached to his feet, or nearly so.
Said boy was taken up in March last by
Charles Cox, near the mouth of Cole's
creek, from whom he made his escape, and
has not been heard of from that time to the
present.

Peter was brought to this state by Franklin and Ballard, last fall, of whom I purchased him. There is no doubt but that he
has denied his own as well as his owner's
name; if so, he is easily frightened by the
whip, and may be made to tell the truth readily. I will give the above reward of twenty
dollars to any person delivering said boy to
me, or securing him in any jail, so that I
can get him again.

                                    P. NOLAND.
Near Rodney, May 27.   16—tf
☞ The *Natchez Courier* will please insert the above *three* times, and forward account to this office.

and details about the lives of those who have not been able to have their narratives or details about their lives shared. These advertisements would typically include specifics and physical descriptions of these individuals, their skills, their literacy level, and where they may be traveling, as well as a reward for the recapture and return of the person described in the ad; however, teachers can use these ads as learning tools to bring life to the individuals most affected by slavery, the slaves themselves (Costa & Doyle, 2004; Lewis, 2016; Singer, 2007). Joshua Rothman, a historian at the University of Alabama, notes that the owners "wanted to provide as much detail about their appearance, their life story, how they carried themselves, what they were wearing . . . Each one of these things is sort of a little biography" (Lewis, 2016, para. 3). The fact that slavery existed and that these advertisements depict human beings as property is without a doubt morally repugnant (Costa & Doyle, 2004; Singer, 2007). It is vital that teachers address this frankly with students, avoid trivializing what individuals endured, and make sure that they are fully clear as to the original intent of these sources. Students can use them today to better understand the time period and, in this case, a piece of literature. Costa and Doyle (2004) urge teachers to consider making this moral dilemma an intentional part of instruction:

> Many people in the 18th and early 19th centuries accepted slavery and did not find it offensive, although

there was a growing campaign to end the practice. It is important and challenging to balance a message of modern morality with an accurate historical context. (Costa & Doyle, pp. 8–9)

SCRUTINIZING THE FUNDAMENTAL SOURCE(S)

For this investigation framed by the SOURCES Framework for Teaching With Primary and Secondary Sources, *Huckleberry Finn* is used as the fundamental source. Students can read the entire text or be provided with excerpts that illustrate how the author, Mark Twain, portrayed one of the main characters, Jim (www.gutenberg.org/files/76/76-h/76-h.htm; Figure 7.4), and what one might be led to believe about slaves and African Americans at this point in American history. While the students read the text, there may be questions that arise and investigations to be had, but I would suggest that the inquiry be framed by the essential question, "How appropriate is the portrayal of Jim and other African Americans in *Huckleberry Finn*?" In this investigation, runaway slave ads are the main sources for analysis, but many other primary sources exist that will help students to understand people who lived during this time period. Depictions of the individuals in these ads were generally fairly representative of who they were, as noted in *Huckleberry Finn* about a slave ad posted about Jim: "The reading was all about Jim and just described him to a dot." (p. 171).

Figure 7.4. Jim and the Ghost

JIM AND THE GHOST.

ORGANIZING THOUGHTS

As students organize their thoughts, they should be asked to carefully examine the portrayal of the various actors in this narrative; however, they should be most aware of Mark Twain's presentation of Jim (www.gutenberg.org/files/76/76-h/76-h.htm#c12-101; Figure 7.5). Students may inadvertently determine that Jim is not intelligent, is easily fooled, and is overly superstitious, as this is a typical impression after a superficial read of the novel by those who do not pick up on nuanced messages found in the text. Others may think that Jim falls into a traditional stereotypical role of a character in a slave narrative and see Jim as happy, simple, childlike, and contented. Some readers may even see him as "free," even though Jim does not live in a world in which he is free, and due to the way in which the narrative is constructed, students may not even realize that Jim does not receive the proper recognition and respect that he deserves as a human being or rights as a citizen of the United States. Those who read the text more carefully or who have developed a deeper level of schema may believe that Jim has great knowledge of the natural world, has a family and holds deep commitments to them, that there was indeed a need to run away, that he does not actually experience freedom, and possibly that Jim even serves as surrogate father to Huck. Although some of the students' thoughts may be

Figure 7.5. Jim: Oh! Lordy, Lordy!

misguided or unintentional, it is important for them to discuss their under-standings and for teachers to be aware of these poorly developed understand-ings and misconceptions. This is an example of where primary and secondary sources can be so powerful, as they do not always have to be used to support the narratives encountered but can refute potentially incorrect or misguided ideas presented in instruction, in what students read in popular literature, or through various media outlets. Sources often can help students understand a different perspective or can dispel misunderstandings. Additionally, these skills and way of thinking will greatly benefit them in everyday life as they navigate various perspectives and narratives presented to them through traditional and social media outlets and will make them more critical consumers and participatory citizens (Faraon et al., 2020; McGrew et al., 2017; Thomas, 2020).

UNDERSTANDING THE CONTEXT

Teachers can easily utilize what was learned from the *Organizing Thoughts* stage to help them structure the *Understanding the Context* phase. There are numer-ous print and digital resources that can be used to help students put *Huckle-berry Finn* in its proper context. As noted earlier, autobiographies by former slaves such as Frederick Douglass and Solomon Northup, as well as sources from the Federal Writers' Project, can greatly add to the understandings stu-dents have developed. They would also benefit from reading portions of Alex Haley's 1976 novel *Roots: The Saga of an American Family* and/or from watching selected pieces of the television miniseries based on the novel. Teaching Tol-erance, a project of the Southern Poverty Law Center, also provides a pleth-ora of resources on its website, such as lessons, content, and videos focusing on teaching "hard history" and slavery (www.tolerance.org/frameworks/teaching-hard-history/american-slavery/k-5-framework?fbclid=IwAR1f3Nw2MC-7-JZtPooeJJmJWI_ubyx7yZ8cwuqavGkw309-VX9BV8ohhrM[a]). On this site, students can watch short video clips, such as one from scholar Annette Gordon-Reed, as she discusses the challenges of using texts created by enslav-ers to understand the lives of enslaved people. Other scholars provide short videos that will help to humanize the individuals affected and show ways in which "enslaved people resisted the efforts of their enslavers to reduce them to commodities in both revolutionary and everyday ways" and how these people "worked to maintain cultural traditions while building new ones that sustain communities and impact the larger world." As teachers work through how best to allow students to better understand this time in history, which is such a critical and controversial topic, they should try to avoid whitewashing history. A resource such as Teaching *Huck Finn* Without Regret (www.tolerance.org/magazine/teaching-huck-finn-without-regret[b]) can help them conceptualize the best way to organize this investigation.

READING BETWEEN THE LINES

At this stage in the investigation, students are asked to think about what they know about the subject and to return to the fundamental source to see how their understandings have evolved and changed. For this inquiry, students should go back to *Huckleberry Finn* and determine what their thoughts are regarding the story presented, especially comments and characterizations of Jim, and should critically examine how the author portrayed Jim and other enslaved individuals. Far too often, students are expected to read, ingest, and be ready to regurgitate information presented in textbooks and literature. It is important for students to have a healthy and respectable level of skepticism and questioning about anything with which they are being presented. These skills are vital to successful learning and inquiry and are at the heart of what they need to become engaged critical thinkers and consumers within a modern republic. For this investigation, students should be encouraged to think critically about the narrative presented in *Huckleberry Finn* and to determine how they might go about corroborating and refuting the statements found in the text. They should pay special attention to the portrayal of Jim and how this might be reconciled with thoughts and narratives about what life was like during this period in American history and what individuals, especially those who were enslaved, might have experienced; consider their levels of intelligence and creativity; and create a better understanding of the uniqueness of a diverse set of individuals affected by the deplorable institution of slavery.

CORROBORATING AND REFUTING

By now, students will have started to develop a narrative around the essential question, "How appropriate is the portrayal of Jim and other African Americans in *Huckleberry Finn*?" Primary sources, especially runaway slave advertisements in this case, are a powerful resource to utilize as students work to corroborate and refute their understandings regarding what is presented in *Huckleberry Finn*. Beyond just the portrayal of Jim (www.gutenberg.org/files/76/76-h/76-h.htm#c14-112; Figure 7.6), students should try to create a narrative or thesis on how African Americans were characterized during this period in history. Runaway slave ads can be found in a variety of places. Through projects conducted by scholars at the Virginia Center for Digital History, Colonial Williamsburg, University of North Carolina Greensboro, the National Humanities Center, and other similar projects, a number of these advertisements have been digitized and made available online and, additionally, a unique and wide selection of ads can be found within newspapers for sale on eBay (see Chapter 11).

Figure 7.6. Jim: The Story of "Sollermun"

In trying to answer the essential question about the portrayal of African Americans versus what may have been reality, students can gain from these runaway slave ads a better understanding of the capabilities of individuals, although enslaved, and their levels of intelligence, creativity, and humanistic characteristics. These ads can easily be found from times spanning the 18th and 19th centuries. In an example from the *Virginia Gazette* (Williamsburg, Virginia) (www2.vcdh.virginia.edu/gos/search/relatedAd.php?adFile=rg68.xml& adId=v1768090293; Figure 7.7), printed on September 22, 1768, students can read about a man named Peter Deadfoot, who clearly displayed great ingenuity, creativity, skill, and pride.

They can also read about Jack in the *Virginia Gazette* (Williamsburg, Virginia) (www2.vcdh.virginia.edu/gos/search/relatedAd.php?adFile=rg67.xml& adId=v1767030207; Figure 7.8) from March 19, 1767, to help bring to life individuals who were so brutally dehumanized.

Another example is of David, who had an ad published about him in the *Virginia Gazette* (Williamsburg, Virginia) (www.newspapers.com/clip/7450569 /5_nov_1772_thomas_gaskins_runaway_slave; Figure 7.9) on November 5, 1772. Students can begin to get a sense that these human beings who were described as property had unique qualities, skills, and levels of intelligence not conveyed in literature such as *Huckleberry Finn*.

Another advertisement, from August 12, 1773, includes a description of Jem, from Antigua, in which the writer describes how "he talks French, can read and write and dresses and shaves tolerably well. . . . He is an artful cunning Fellow" (https://www.google.com/url?sa=t&rct=j&q=&esrc=s&source=web&cd=&

Figure 7.7. *Virginia Gazette* (Rind, pub.), Williamsburg, September 22, 1768

RAN away last April, from one of the subscriber"s quarters in Loudoun, (where he had been a short time sawing) a Mulatto slave belonging to Samuel Selden, jun. named Peter Deadfoot, though it is supposed he has changed his name, as he the day before attempted to pass for a freeman, and had got as far as Noland's ferry, on his way to Philadelphia, by a forged pass, in which he was called William Swann. He is a tall, slim, clean limbed, active, genteel, handsome fellow, with broad shoulders; about 22 years of age, a dark Mulatto, with a nose rather flat than otherwise, very sensible, and smooth tongued; but is apt to speak quick, swear, and with dreadful curses upon himself, in defence of his innocence, if taxed with a fault, even when guilty; which may be easily discovered, by any person"s taxing him with being run away. He is an indifferent shoemaker, a good butcher, ploughman, and carter; an excellent sawyer, and waterman, understands breaking oxen well, and is one of the best scythemen, either with or without a cradle, in America; in short, he is so ingenious a fellow, that he can turn his hand to anything; he has a great share of pride, though he is very obliging, is extremely fond of dress; and though his holiday clothes were taken from him, when he first attempted to get off, yet, as he has probably passed for a freeman, I make no doubt he has supplied himself with others, as such a fellow would readily get employment; it has been reported that he was seen on board a vessel in York river, near York town; but for my own part, I suspect that he is either in Prince William county, Charles county in Maryland (in both which places he has relations) or in the neighbourhood of Winchester. Whoever apprehends the said slave, and conveys him to me in Stafford county, shall receive, if taken within ten miles of my house, Five Pounds; if above fifty miles, Ten Pounds; and if above one hundred miles, Twenty Pounds reward, besides what the law allows. THOMSON MASON.

Figure 7.8. *Virginia Gazette* (Purdie & Dixon, pub.), Williamsburg, March 19, 1767

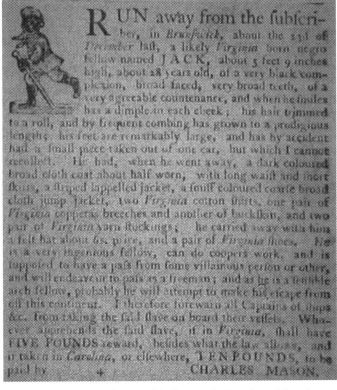

JACK, about 5 feet 9 inches high, about 28 years old, of a very black complexion, broad faced, very broad teeth, of a very agreeable countenance, and when he smiles has a dimple in each cheek; his hair trimmed to a roll and by frequent combing has grown to a prodigious length; his feet are remarkably large, and has by accident had a small piece taken out of one ear, but which I cannot recollect . . . He is a very ingenious fellow, can do coopers work, and is supposed to have a pass from some villainous person or other, and will endeavor to pass as a freeman; and as he is a sensible arch fellow, probably he will attempt to make his escape from off this continent . . .

cad=rja&uact=8&ved=2ahUKEwjRyu3Lz9zrAhXhqlkKHbgLAEwQFjABegQ-IARAC&url=http%3A%2F%2Fnationalhumanitiescenter.org%2F-pds%2Fmaai%2Fenslavement%2Ftext8%2Fvirginiarunawayads.pdf&usg=AOvVaw3_o1Xt1kGONWrlABE5j-_H[c]). A description of Billy, from April 14, 1774, describes a 20-year-old man who is "five Feet nine Inches high, stout and strong made, has a remarkable Swing in his Walk. . . . From his Ingenuity, he is capable of doing almost any sort of Business, and for some Years past has been chiefly employed as a Founder, a Stone Mason, and a Miller, as Occasion required; one of which Trades, I imagine, he will, in the Character of a Freeman" (http://www2.vcdh.virginia.edu/gos/search/relatedAd.php?adFile=rg74.xml&adId=v1774040986[d]).

Students can also read about Scott in the *Weekly State Journal* (Raleigh, North Carolina) from July 28, 1862, that he is "about twenty years old, very

> **TEN POUNDS REWARD,**
>
> RUN away from the Subfcriber, in *Northumberland*, on *Wednefday* the 14th of *October*, a very likely young *Virginia* born Negro Man named DAVID, of a yellowish Complexion, and about five Feet five Inches high; had on when he went off an Ofnabrug Shirt, a Pair of Purple *Virginia* Cloth Breeches lined with white Linen, a Pair of Rolls Breeches over them, and a Fearnought Jacket with Horn Buttons. He carried with him a brown coloured Kerfey Jacket, a blue and white *Virginia* Cloth One with coarfe Ofnabrug Pockets, brown and white Linen Shirts, and fundry other Clothes which I cannot well deferibe; but, as he is a very cunning artful Fellow, I imagine he will fell and fwap his Clothes as may fuit him. Though his Hair is of the Negro Kind, he keeps it very high and well combed; but, as he wants to be free, I imagine he will cut it off, and get a Wig to alter and difguife himfelf. He had with him thirty or forty Shillings in Silver Money, and a Brafs Medal with the Image of our prefent King and Queen on it, which he will endeavour to pafs for Gold. He can read pretty well, and I make no Doubt will endeavour to pafs for a Freeman and get himfelf a forged Pafs, and endeavour for fome foreign Part, either by getting on Board of fome Veffel or ftealing fome Gentleman's Horfe and make for *Carolina*. He has always been my Waiting Man when I went from home, and is a good Waiter, Driver, and Hoftler, underftands fomething of Gardening, of combing and dreffing Wigs and Hair, can plough, work at the Hoe and Axe very well, and is, on the Whole, a very clever active brifk Fellow. Whoever will apprehend the faid Runaway, and bring him home to me, or fecure him in any Jail in the Colony, fo that I get him, fhall have FIVE POUNDS Reward, and reafonable Charges allowed; if out of the Colony TEN POUNDS, and reafonable Charges for bringing him home.
>
>   (1)   THOMAS GASKINS.
>
> *N. B.* He is fufpected to have carried with him a Drab coloured Sailor's Jacket with Slafh Sleeves, Leather Buttons on the Sleeves, if not on the Breaft, and lined through with red and white Swanfkin; alfo a Pair of old white Plufh Breeches, which are miffing.

Figure 7.9. 5 Nov 1772 Thomas Gaskins, Runaway Slave

. . . a very likely young Virginia born Negro Man named DAVID, of a yellowish Complexion, and about five Feet five Inches high . . . Though his Hair is of the Negro Kind, he keeps it very high and well combed; but, as he wants to be free, I imagine he will cut it off, and get a Wig to alter and disguise himself. He had with him thirty or forty Shillings in Silver Money, and a Brass Medal with the Image of our present King and Queen on it, which he will endeavor to pass for Gold. He can read pretty well, and I make no Doubt will endeavour to pass for a Freeman and get himself a forged Pass, and endeavor for some foreign Part, either by getting on Board of some Vessel or stealing some Gentleman's Horse and make for Carolina. He has always been my Waiting Man when I went from home, and is a good Waiter, Driver, and Hostler, understands something of Gardening, of combing and dressing Wigs and Hair, can plow, work at the Hoe and Axe very well, and is, on the Whole, a very clever active brisk Fellow.

bright mulatto . . . usually smiles when talked to . . . he is a likely, quick and active boy" (libcdm1.uncg.edu/cdm/singleitem/collection/RAS/id/4001/rec/31ᶜ). One can read an advertisement, in the *Weekly Raleigh Register* on September 8, 1856, about "a servant girl named MARGARET . . . said girl is a bright mulatto . . . she is a good looking and intelligent girl, and prepossessing in her manners" (libcdm1.uncg.edu/cdm/singleitem/collection/RAS/id/5568/rec/35[f]).

Students can also read about family members who escaped together, such as "Sally is about thirty-four years of age, very black, white teeth & of common size. Her child Rosetta is a very bright mulatto girl. About eight years of age, with very straight hair"—Raleigh, April 6, 1826—*Star and North Carolina State Gazette* (libcdm1.uncg.edu/cdm/singleitem/collection/RAS/id/117/rec/11[g]). Another advertisement is for three people, possibly a family, and is found in the *Roanoke Advocate* from January 25, 1832.

JOE is a Blacksmith, about 33 years old, not very dark, with a heavy head, has a down look when spoken to and is about 6 feet high, inclined to be slender.

TEMPY is a small woman rather dark and is about 25 years old, she is quite an intelligent and genteel looking negro.

NEEDHAM is a smart boy about 9 or 10 years old and can read and write. (libcdm1.uncg.edu/cdm/singleitem/collection/RAS/id/189/rec/10[h])

There are also examples of groups of individuals who ran away, like those described in an ad in the *Raleigh Register and North Carolina Weekly Advertiser* on May 1, 1816.

TOM and BEN. Tom is a Blacksmith, about 23 years of age, five feet six or seven inches high, well made, complexion tolerably dark and grim countenance, his hair combed up before, with which he has taken much care. Ben is also a Blacksmith, about 19 years old, about five feet seven or eight inches high, complexion a little yellow, and of a pleasant countenance. They are sensible and intelligent negroes. (libcdm1.uncg.edu/cdm/singleitem/collection/RAS/id/60/rec/6[i])

Overall, the goal for this investigation is to help students realize that these were human beings, individuals with their own skills, qualities, and characteristics, and despite the typical characterization, many of these individuals, like Sterling (September 10, 1839), were "very shrewd and intelligent" (libcdm1.uncg.edu/cdm/singleitem/collection/RAS/id/1763/rec/46[j]).

Other sources can be found on the websites of the National Humanities Center (nationalhumanitiescenter.org/pds/maai/enslavement/text8/virginia runawayads.pdf[k]), the Freedom on the Move project at Cornell University (freedomonthemove.org[l]), the North Carolina Runaway Slave Advertisements project at the University of North Carolina Greensboro (libcdm1.uncg.edu/cdm/landingpage/collection/RAS[m]), and even on eBay (www.ebay.com[n]) (see Chapter 11).

ESTABLISHING A PLAUSIBLE NARRATIVE

In order for the students to properly dissect what they have read in *Huckleberry Finn*, related literature, and primary sources like the runaway slave ads, convey their understandings in a concise manner to the teacher, and respond to the essential question for the investigation, "How appropriate is the portrayal of Jim and other African Americans in *Huckleberry Finn*?," I suggest that they be assigned to write a kind of "letter to the editor," responding to what they have read and describing how they have come to visualize some of those individuals who were enslaved. Other final assessment pieces can be utilized, but with this assignment, I suggest that students should pull excepts from *Huckleberry Finn* and other literature and provide responses based on the runaway slave ads and other sources reviewed in the form of a response letter. This will help to reemphasize the importance of utilizing data and sources to corroborate narratives and personal arguments and successfully consider, and possibly defend, perspectives that may differ from what is being presented in literature, as well as in traditional and social media. Additionally, it will build a sense of agentic power within the students as they realize that, in addition to many other ways to responding to social, moral, or political injustice, they can write letters to the editor or construct editorial commentaries when they feel the need to act.

SUMMARIZING FINAL THOUGHTS

There are many different ways in which a teacher can approach the last stage, *Summarizing Final Thoughts*. For this investigation, it might be useful for students to think about the process, to review what they learned, and to consider what questions still exist. Then they can pair up with a classmate and share their thoughts regarding the depictions of African Americans, such as Jim, in literature from this time period. The investigation can conclude with a whole-class discussion about what they learned about the individuals impacted by slavery, about themselves and their learning, and about how they best obtain new knowledge. There should also be conversation about how their understandings of who enslaved people were evolved as they progressed through this investigation and how those sources impacted their ways of thinking, as well as how people are still discriminated against in contemporary society, how sources portray them today, and methods for combating ignorance demonstrated by individuals and misinformation being disseminated through traditional and social media outlets.

CONCLUSION

Through this investigation, students are given the opportunity to examine a piece of literature, *The Adventures of Huckleberry Finn*; determine how accurate the portrayal of a literary character is in comparison to actual individuals who lived during that period; and respond to an essential question, "How appropriate is the portrayal of Jim and other African Americans in *Huckleberry Finn*?" They are able to utilize primary sources, in this case runaway slave advertisements, as they use skills of corroboration and refutation to work toward creating a picture of the diversity of intellect, character, and talents of enslaved individuals in the United States during 18th- and 19th-century America.

QR CODES FOR LINKS IN TEXT

CHAPTER 8

An Examination of Ciphers
An Application of the SOURCES Framework

The examination of ciphers and codes can allow students to grapple with "real-world mathematical and computational thinking skills" (Apfeldorf, 2018, para. 1). A cipher is a code or a method of transforming text in order to hide the original message's meaning. An example of a cipher that has been used for over 500 years would be a cipher disk (upload.wikimedia.org/wikipedia/commons/b/b5/CipherDisk2000.jpg; Figure 8.1). Cipher disks, rotation algorithms, or Caesar ciphers rely on mathematical methods where the user transposes each of the letters in a text-based message to another letter. Basically, this is done by assigning each letter in the alphabet a new letter designation based on how many positions each letter should change when decoding a message. Using the cipher, the reader will change the letters to other letters by rotating or changing the location of a letter within the alphabet. For example,

Figure 8.1. Cipher Disk

someone using the "rotational 13" (ROT13) method would replace each letter in a message with the letter that comes 13 spots later in the alphabet, so that it results in A=N, B=O, etc. The user needs to know only the algorithm or the number of spots in the alphabet to move in order to encrypt or decrypt the message (Watson, 2017). In this investigation, structured through the use of the SOURCES Framework for Teaching With Primary and Secondary Sources, students are asked to examine a series of ciphers utilized at various times in history to determine hidden messages and consider the level of effectiveness of using codes and ciphers.

SCRUTINIZING THE FUNDAMENTAL SOURCE(S)

To begin, students can easily see how the Caesar method works on rot13.com, a website that allows for the decryption of rotational algorithm messages. On the Cryptii website (cryptii.com; seen in Figure 8.2), the user may choose from a variety of ciphers, including more complex ones such as the Enigma, Morse, or Bacon methods. For example, one may enter the message "V ybir gb grnpu jvgu cevznel fbheprf!" on either website and set it to decrypt the message using the Caesar/rotational 13 procedure and quickly learn that my intended message is "I love to teach with primary sources!" (Figure 8.2). Teachers should allow students to try out different methods, create encrypted messages, and share messages with classmates for them to decrypt. Depending on the student level and ability, teachers can assign students to create encrypted messages that necessitate the use of more complex mathematical operations and equations.

To pique student interest with a real example from American history, teachers should utilize the cipher provided by Thomas Jefferson to Meriwether Lewis on April 20, 1803, as Lewis left on his historic journey across the United States with William Clark and the Corps of Discovery (www.loc.gov/resource/

Figure 8.2. Cryptii Website—Using the Rotational 13 Method

mtj1.028_0175_0176/?st=gallery; Figure 8.3). It is unclear whether the cypher was used by Lewis or Clark during the expedition, but it is clear that secrecy was vital to this mission and that both parties understood the need for the use of codes and ciphers. Students should be instructed to examine the cipher and to work on creating a message to a classmate. The classmate can create a message as well, and they can be exchanged for deciphering. More advanced

Figure 8.3. Thomas Jefferson to Meriwether Lewis, April 20, 1803, Cipher

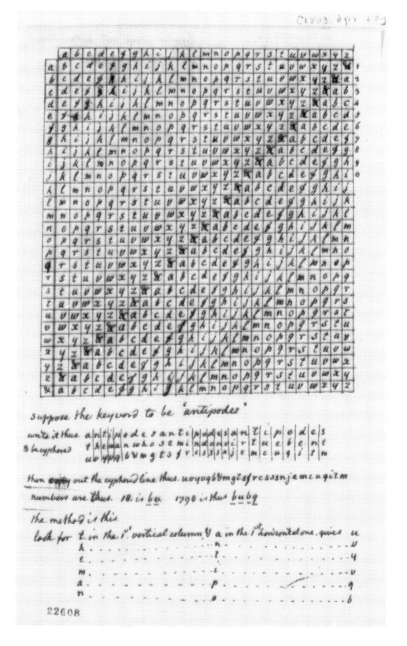

students could combine the Jefferson cipher with the Caesar cipher by using the Jefferson cipher as well as shifting the letter value by a constant alphabetical value such as five. As students are encrypting and decrypting messages, they should think critically about the advantages and disadvantages of using ciphers and codes. Apfeldorf (2018) suggests that, in order to increase interest and impact, teachers need to have students focus on, utilize, and reflect upon "real-world," geographic, and travel-related situations and the communication technologies employed at various times throughout history, such as those possibly used by George Washington, Thomas Jefferson, Meriwether Lewis and William Clark, American Civil War officers, Navajo code talkers during the Second World War, and others needing to utilize ciphers at different times in history.

ORGANIZING THOUGHTS

At this stage of the inquiry investigation, students should think about the ciphers used, especially the one utilized by Thomas Jefferson, Meriwether Lewis, and William Clark. They should compile a list of situations when and where a cipher might be useful and even necessary. Students should think, pair, and share their ideas, prior to whole-class discussion about the use of ciphers. As they move forward, they will want to focus on the essential question, "How would you develop the most secure cipher for . . . ?" Allow students to complete the essential question with something that is extremely important to them personally. During the last part of this stage of the framework, students should think about what they do not understand about ciphers, what questions exist, and what more they want to know about the use of ciphers and codes throughout history.

UNDERSTANDING THE CONTEXT

To help students understand how ciphers work, why they are used, and how to develop ciphers of their own, several wonderful books can help them build contextual understanding, such as:

Daigneau, J. (2019). *Code cracking for kids: Secret communications throughout history, with 21 codes and ciphers*. Chicago Review Press.
Janeczko, P. B. (2004). *Top secret: A handbook of codes, ciphers, and secret writing*. Candlewick Press.
Johnson, B. (2013). *Break the code: Cryptography for beginners*. Dover Publications.

Additionally, there are numerous helpful videos on YouTube, and the Khan Academy website provides an instructional course on cryptography, including the use of the Caesar cipher, the Enigma, and other interesting approaches (www.khanacademy.org/computing/computer-science/cryptography/crypt/v/intro-to-cryptography[a]).

If students want more information about the Lewis and Clark Expedition, PBS's Lewis & Clark: The Journey of the Corps of Discovery (www.pbs.org/lewisandclark) is quite useful and serves as a nice complement to the Ken Burns documentary about this historic voyage. The Library of Congress, on its Rivers, Edens, Empires: Lewis & Clark and the Revealing of America page (www.loc.gov/exhibits/lewisandclark/lewis-multimedia.html[b]), offers a variety of important content, multimedia presentations, and sources. Students who want more information about the cipher used by Jefferson and Clark should visit the Monticello website and look specifically at the section focusing on the cipher (www.monticello.org/thomas-jefferson/louisiana-lewis-clark/preparing-for-the-expedition/coded-messages/jefferson-s-cipher-for-meriwether-lewis). For fun, students should also look at Meriwether Lewis' estimate for the expenses necessary to properly conduct the expedition (www.loc.gov/resource/mtj1.028_0183_0184; Figure 8.4).

READING BETWEEN THE LINES

Now that students have a clear understanding of what ciphers are and how they work, they should revisit the fundamental source, Jefferson's cipher for

"Recapitulation of an estimate of the sum necessary to carry into effect the Miss[issippi] expedition"

Mathematical Instruments	$ 217
Arms & Accoutrements extraordinary	81
Camp Equipage	255
Medicine & packing	55
Means of transportation	430
Indian presents	696
Provisions extraordinary	224
Materials for making up the various articles into portable packs	55
For the pay of hunters guides & Interpreters	300
In silver coin to defray the expenses of the party from Nashville to the last white settlement on the Missisourie	100
Contingencies	87
Total	$2,500

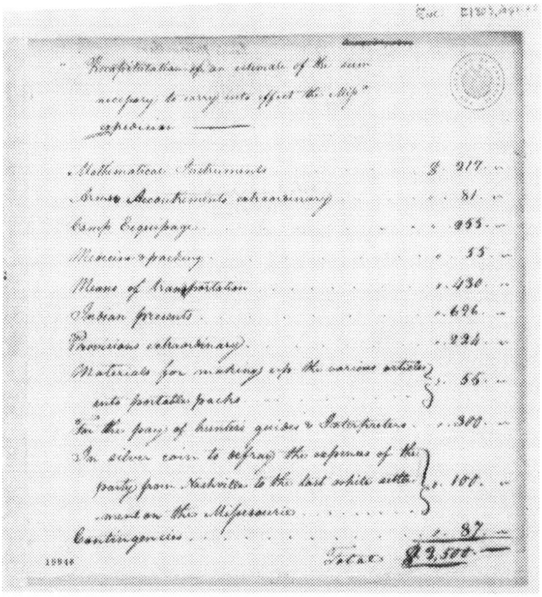

Figure 8.4. Meriwether Lewis, April 20, 1803, Expedition Estimate

Meriwether Lewis (Figure 8.3). Students should think more critically about why President Jefferson felt that a cipher was necessary and about how it might have been used. They should also consider possibilities for how ciphers would be utilized in contemporary society and life.

CORROBORATING AND REFUTING

Once students are comfortable with utilizing Jefferson's cipher, they should think about the mathematics involved in this process and should utilize this cipher while expressing statements as mathematical equations (Apfeldorf, 2018). They can begin with more basic alphanumerical ciphers, such as A=0, B=1, Z=25, etc., and construct a key that would allow the user to determine to the corresponding letter. Then more complex equations can be constructed, especially as students begin to engage with more advanced algebraic equations and modular mathematics. As they move forward, students should focus on the essential question of "How would you develop the most secure cipher for . . . ?"

For more complex and creative approaches, teachers can also create break-out boxes that utilize ciphers in the process. A breakout box, like an escape room, is an instructional approach where students must work together to solve a series of problems, and ultimately break into a box that provides the solution to a mystery. Proper use of this approach makes cooperative learning, collaboration, and the use of ciphers necessary for students to find success, and an added benefit is that this approach can be quite fun for students as well.

For a real-life situation where ciphers were used, students can be directed to the Veterans History Project of the Library of Congress (www.loc.gov/vets[c]) to learn about two of the women (Ann Caracristi and Ann Ellicott Madeira) (blogs .loc.gov/folklife/files/2018/02/Koczela_91889.jpeg; Figure 8.5) who worked decrypting enemy codes during the Second World War. They can begin by listening to several excerpts from interviews, such as:

- How Caracristi was recruited and what her training was like (0:59 to 8:09; memory.loc.gov/diglib/vhp/story/loc.natlib. afc2001001.30844/afc2001001_030844_mv0001001_640x480_800. stream?start=59&clipid=d17016e106[d])
- Caracristi high points and key successes (3:30 to 6:23; memory.loc. gov/diglib/vhp/story/loc.natlib.afc2001001.30844/afc2001001_ 030844_mv0002001_640x480_800.stream?start=210&clipid= d17016e236[e])
- Caracristi on secrecy and the mix of colleagues (23:12 to 26:40; memory.loc.gov/diglib/vhp/story/loc.natlib.afc2001001.30844/ afc2001001_030844_mv0001001_640x480_800.stream?start= 1392&clipid=d17016e171[f])

Figure 8.5. Photograph of a WAVE Decoding Unit Stationed at the Naval Communications Command Annex, Washington, DC, 1945

Ruth Koczela Collection, Veterans History Project, American Folklife Center, AFC2001/001/91889.

- Why Caracristi left the service, then came back (0:05 to 2:13; memory.loc.gov/diglib/vhp/story/loc.natlib.afc2001001.30844/ afc2001001_030844_mv0002001_640x480_800. stream?start=5&clipid=d17016e220[g])
- How Madeira was recruited by the Navy, even before Pearl Harbor (0:45-1:56; memory.loc.gov/diglib/vhp/story/loc.natlib.afc2001001. 07563/afc2001001_007563_sr0001001.stream?start=45&clipid= d21968e104[h])
- Madeira's description of how certain Japanese codes were cracked (5:30 to 8:57; memory.loc.gov/diglib/vhp/story/loc.natlib.afc 2001001.07563/?loclr=blogflt[i]).

After listening to the excerpts, students can write a diary or log entry as a codebreaker, detailing the job responsibilities, expectations, and need to be secretive in a role such as the one undertaken by Ann Caracristi and Ann Ellicott Madeira. Students should also spend time creating and deciphering a variety of codes and ciphers, such as Morse Code and a Pigpen Cipher (www.

youtube.com/watch?v=s5XRTcLYy40[j]), that were used in real life by people needing to keep information secret.

ESTABLISHING A PLAUSIBLE NARRATIVE

There are many possibilities for how the students might create a plausible narrative to respond to the essential question, "How would you develop the most secure cipher for . . . ?"

This would also be an excellent opportunity for students to develop a creative story or fiction based on a spy's use of a cipher. I would suggest that students be required to complete this assessment piece as a spy story or a graphic novel. Other effective options would be to have the students respond to the essential question in the form of a diary of a code writer/breaker, and even write the entries utilizing the cipher that they developed, or as a series of letters home to a friend or loved one, once again using the cipher. To successfully complete the assessment, I would expect that the narrative include why the cipher was needed, how it was constructed, how it was employed, and ways in which it resembled other codes and ciphers used in the past.

SUMMARIZING FINAL THOUGHTS

During the final stage of the SOURCES framework, *Summarizing Final Thoughts*, students are encouraged to examine their thoughts regarding the learning process and how they acquired new knowledge, in this case about ciphers. Students would benefit greatly from reading or hearing the narratives of classmates and learning how each individual saw ways in which a cipher would assist them in keeping personal information secure. They once again should critically think and examine the value of using codes and ciphers and determine various situations in which they would be useful.

CONCLUSION

In this investigation, students are given an opportunity to think critically about the use of codes and ciphers by examining historical and contemporary uses of ciphers, as well as how they might use a cipher in their own lives. To begin, students have an opportunity to analyze the fundamental source: the cipher provided by Thomas Jefferson to Meriwether Lewis. Then they have the opportunity to examine various codes and ciphers while considering, throughout this investigation, the essential question of "How would you develop the most secure cipher for . . . ?."

QR CODES FOR LINKS IN TEXT

a.
b.
c.
d.
e.

f.
g.
h.
i.
j.

CHAPTER 9

Are We Alone in the Universe?
An Application of the SOURCES Framework

One of the most valuable online repositories of primary sources, even for science teachers, is the Library of Congress. Among the library's digital collections is "Finding Our Place in the Cosmos: From Galileo to Sagan and Beyond." This collection of artifacts explores various models of the universe and how they have changed over time; different ideas of what life may exist on other worlds; and Carl Sagan's place in the tradition of science. The collection of manuscripts, rare books, celestial atlases, newspaper articles, sheet music, and movie posters includes perspectives of noted scientists such as Carl Sagan, the astrophysicist, writer, television personality, and professor who explained astronomy, science, and math for the everyday person to understand.

Teachers can utilize this collection and associated resources to construct integrated curricula so students can engage with sources through the SOURCES Framework for Teaching With Primary and Secondary Sources and address essential questions like "Are we alone in the universe?" Through this investigation, learners will be able to explore various perspectives and then create and defend their own hypotheses or thesis statements based on available sources from the collection and beyond. The "Finding Our Place in the Cosmos" collection is most appropriate for middle grades through high school, though some manuscripts and notebooks have concepts and computations that only students with advanced skills would fully understand. However, with proper scaffolding, even these items can help novice learners understand perspectives on life beyond Earth without having a full comprehension of the more complex computations. As presenting students with the vast collection provided by the Library of Congress can overwhelm even the more knowledgeable student, teachers will want to provide students with only selected parts of the collection to assess and analyze. This is where the SOURCES framework and the SOURCES Framework Analysis Sheet (Figure 1.13) will help the teacher structure learning and allow students to properly progress through the inquiry process.

SCRUTINIZING THE FUNDAMENTAL SOURCE(S)

Since the focus of this lesson is on Carl Sagan's perspective concerning our place in the universe and the possibility of extraterrestrial life, an introductory source to be shared with the students should be something that would be considered fundamental to understanding this and would allow learners' understanding of the essential question, "Are we alone in the universe?" For this investigation, I would suggest introducing two sources to the students. The first is an image taken of Earth (www.nasa.gov/feature/jpl/pale-blue-dot -revisited; Figure 9.1), at Sagan's suggestion, by *Voyager 1* on February 14, 1990. As the Voyager spacecraft reached the edges of our solar system, about 4 billion miles away, engineers took one last look at Earth and captured this iconic image of our "Pale Blue Dot." Looking at this image, one is able to see Earth at the center of scattered light rays. This is a result of the image having been taken so close to the Sun. In this image, Earth appears as a tiny point of light. For the 30th anniversary of the capturing of this image, NASA's Jet Propulsion Laboratory in Pasadena, California, published an updated version of the *Pale Blue Dot*. The updated image uses modern image-processing software and techniques to add clarity. Along with this source, teachers should play an audio recording of Sagan entitled *Pale Blue Dot* (www.loc.gov/item/cosmos000110[a]), which is also the title of a Sagan book. This four-and-a-half-minute recording, which expresses Sagan's thoughts about the *Voyager* spacecraft and our place in the universe, is a perfect fundamental source to be utilized to begin the investigation. I would suggest that students first listen to the recording individually and then be given an opportunity to think, pair, and share their thoughts; sharing could be done in groups or as a whole class. While listening to the audio clip for the first time, they should use a primary source analysis sheet, such as the SOURCES Analysis Sheet (Figure 1.12) or the observe, reflect, and question primary source analysis tool from the Library of Congress. On the Library's website, they also provide a teacher

Figure 9.1. Pale Blue Dot

guide to assist teachers by providing them with ideas for helping students to analyze audio clips (https://www.loc.gov/programs/teachers/getting-started-with-primary-sources/guides[b]). During this period of time, the teacher should circulate among students and be available to provide support or clarification. After the initial listening and recording of thoughts, the students should group together with one or two classmates, discuss thoughts and questions, and then listen to the recording again after considering the observation questions from the analysis sheet. Students can add to their observations recorded, reflect on what Carl Sagan expressed, and once again contemplate the essential question, "Are we alone in the universe?"

ORGANIZING THOUGHTS

During the second stage of the SOURCES framework, students should discuss the sound recording further and begin to focus on who Sagan was, why they think he made the recording, and how significant they believe Sagan and the recording are to answering the essential question posed for this investigation. The teacher should direct the students to contemplate any questions that they may have after listening to the recording, to discuss them with a classmate, and to write them down so that they can refer to them throughout the investigation. Students should then organize their thoughts, possibly using concept mapping tools (e.g., Mindmeister, Ayao, Miro, or other mind-mapping applications) to help them. Students need to focus their thinking on what they definitely know about the topic of study and what knowledge is still missing in order to begin developing a response to the question, "Are we alone in the universe?"

UNDERSTANDING THE CONTEXT

At this point, students should self-check for content and context comprehension, thinking critically about what prior knowledge they have that is related to the fundamental source (Sagan audio clip). If any of the students know about the life and work of Carl Sagan, SETI (search for extraterrestrial intelligence), Voyager, or general space travel, they can be asked to share their understandings with the class. Students can be assigned to read excerpts from Carl Sagan's work, and teachers can share a piece of children's literature with them, as good children's literature should be used with students of all ages:

- *Star Stuff: Carl Sagan and the Mysteries of the Cosmos* by Stephanie Roth Sisson
- *Carl Went to The Library: The Inspiration of a Young Carl Sagan* by M. J. Mouton

To understand his motivation, the teacher should share Carl Sagan's letter about *Voyager*'s Golden Record, which contains sounds and images selected to portray the diversity of life and culture on Earth and was ultimately intended to be provided to intelligent alien life forms (www.loc.gov/resource/mss85590 .045/?sp=1&r=-0.151,0.946,0.459,0.329,0; Figure 9.2), and NASA's website about the Golden Record (voyager.jpl.nasa.gov/golden-record/whats-on-the -record^c). Students should then discuss various perspectives and avenues for

Figure 9.2. Letter from Carl Sagan to Alan Lomax Regarding the Voyager Golden Record

CORNELL UNIVERSITY
Center for Radiophysics and Space Research

SPACE SCIENCES BUILDING
Ithaca, New York 14853

Telephone (607) 256-4971   Laboratory for Planetary Studies

                                                                 June 6, 1977

Mr. Alan Lomax
215 West 98th Street
Apartment 12E
New York NY   10025

Dear Alan:

I am extremely pleased that you will be able to lend us the benefit of your considerable experience and expertise in ethnomusicology in
the production of the Voyager record.

Voyager I and Voyager II are unmanned deep space probes which will
be launched from Cape Canaveral in August and September, 1977. Their
mission is to examine close-up the major planets, Jupiter, Saturn, and
Uranus, their 20 some odd moons, and the rings of Saturn and Uranus.
After these fly-by observations are performed, the two spacecraft will
be ejected from the solar system, becoming mankind's third and fourth
interstellar space vehicles. The first two such vehicles, Pioneers 10
and 11, were launched some six years ago and contain a 6 x 9 inch gold
anodized aluminium plaque on which is etched some simple scientific information about the location of the Earth and the solar system in the
Milky Way Galaxy, and the moment in the ten billion year history of our
Galaxy when the spacecraft was launched. There are also drawings of a
man and woman. The plaques were a sort of message in a bottle, cast
into the cosmic ocean, in case at some remote epoch in the future an
extraterrestrial civilization were to come upon Pioneer 10 or 11 and
wonder something about its origin.

Voyager permits us to continue on the Pioneer 10 and 11 experience,
but in a much richer way. When NASA asked me to chair a committee to
decide what should be the nature of the Voyager cosmic greeting card,
it soon became clear that much more information could be conveyed in the
same space on a metal mother of a phonograph record than on a plaque of
the same size. Since this is the 100th anniversary of Edison's invention
of the phonograph, a record seems particularly apt. NASA will be launching
on each Voyager a bonded pair of copper mothers containing the equivalent
of four sides of a 12-inch 33-1/3 rpm long playing record. One of these
sides will contain digital scientific information -- largely diagrams
and pictures; a range of human voices, including some especially prepared
at the United Nations and one special greeting by Kurt Waldheim, the U.N.
Secretary General; and a selection of non-musical, non-vocal sounds of

additional investigation and clarification, keeping the ultimate goal of answering the essential question in mind and as the focus of the investigation.

READING BETWEEN THE LINES

Once students have reviewed additional primary and secondary sources for background and contextual information, they should revisit the *Pale Blue Dot* audio clip and their notes regarding their understandings. They should try to determine why Sagan constructed the source as he did and his possible rationale for doing so. The students should think about the source from different perspectives. Teachers can assist with the development of seeking out diverse and different perspectives by creating a classroom environment where it is encouraged to discuss various possible thoughts, questions, and concerns, including choices the author of a source may have faced in constructing it.

CORROBORATING AND REFUTING

At this stage, students are expected to independently conduct research to find other sources to assist in supporting or contradicting the narrative that they are constructing to answer the question, "Are we alone in the universe?" By relying on sources such as "Life on Mars" (chroniclingamerica.loc.gov/lccn/sn98060050/1875-11-19/ed-1/seq-1; Figure 9.3), students will have a basis for their specific arguments and a rationale for their overall response to the essential question. They can use other resources, but they should be encouraged to utilize the three major sections of the Library of Congress's exhibit:

- Modeling the Cosmos (www.loc.gov/collections/finding-our-place-in-the-cosmos-with-carl-sagan/articles-and-essays/modeling-the-cosmos[d])
- Life on Other Worlds: History of the Possibility (www.loc.gov/collections/finding-our-place-in-the-cosmos-with-carl-sagan/articles-and-essays/life-on-other-worlds[e])
- Carl Sagan and the Tradition of Science (www.loc.gov/collections/finding-our-place-in-the-cosmos-with-carl-sagan/articles-and-essays/carl-sagan-and-the-tradition-of-science[f])

Depending upon the amount of class time available, this can be assigned as homework or completed during an in-class day of this investigation; however, students need to collect a variety of sources (primary or secondary) to develop a defendable narrative to answer the essential question. Other sources and

Figure 9.3. Life on Mars

LIFE ON MARS.

A WORLD LIKE OURS, WITH WATER, AIR, HEAT, LIGHT, WINDS, CLOUDS, RAIN, RIV-ULETS, VALLEYS, AND MOUNTAINS.

[Translated for the New York World.]

When twelve years ago I published the first edition of my work "La Pluralité des Mondes," I did hope to see the speedy confirmation which the progress of astronomy would give to my theory in enabling us to touch with the finger as it were, the manifestations of planetary life. On the one hand, the aerolites, those samples of other worlds, have brought in their own substance the elements which play the most important part in life, like oxygen, hydrogen, carbon, chlorure of sodium. The aerolite which fell at Orgueil (Department of Tarn-et-Garonne) brought us coal-like matter, carbures, which, like peat, are due to vegetable remains; that which fell in 1872 at Lance (Loire-et-Choir) brought salt. Aerolites had already brought water under the form of hydrate of oxyde of iron. The worlds from which these debris come do not differ from ours. On the other hand, through the spectral analysis, vapor of water identical with that which produces our fogs, our clouds, and our rains, has been discovered in the planetary atmosphere.

chroniclingamerica.loc.gov/lccn/sn98060050/1875-11-19/ed-1/seq-1

resources that can help them can be found on the NASA website for Exoplanet Exploration: Planets Beyond Our Solar System (exoplanets.nasa.gov[g]), the Institute for Advanced Study (www.ias.edu[h]), the SETI Institute and information about the Drake Equation (www.seti.org/drake-equation-index[i]), and the Planetary Science Institute (www.psi.edu[j]). Through this stage, students are encouraged to utilize and develop 21st-century skills, such as autonomous research and investigative skills. Students need to be given opportunities to investigate questions that do not have easy or definitive answers, so that is why this investigation is a powerful one. Students are asked to critically think about a question that many scientists are contemplating, and one for which there is not a concrete and simple response. Additionally, this is something that many of our students will wonder throughout their lifetimes, and hopefully additional information will emerge that will help them to better respond to the essential question in the years to come.

ESTABLISHING A PLAUSIBLE NARRATIVE

For assessment, students should develop a source-based, plausible narrative to clearly answer the essential question, "Are we alone in the universe?," being sure to include references to the sources they researched and analyzed. They can present in a variety of ways, all of which should be supported with primary and secondary sources:

- Write, act, and record a panel discussion defending and refuting the idea of possible extraterrestrial life. This can be performed as a scripted or unscripted discussion. Students can also be required to post the recording (audio or video) on a course management system for other classmates to view.
- Write a persuasive essay and read it aloud to the class or post it on a course management system, blog, or website.
- Develop a multimedia presentation for or against the existence of extraterrestrial life to present to the class and/or post online or on a course management system.
- Create a blog for classroom students to discuss findings from class and present arguments for and against intelligent life outside Earth.
- Present the Drake equation (used to estimate the probability and number of communicative extraterrestrial civilizations in the Milky Way galaxy) and explain (in detail) how this supports or refutes the idea of intelligent life outside earth.

Creative assessment strategies such as these allow students the flexibility to use their strengths and demonstrate a greater level of comprehension than found with traditional assessment techniques, and replicate methods used by professionals in the field.

SUMMARIZING FINAL THOUGHTS

During the final stage of the SOURCES framework, students should summarize the scope of their investigation, communicate their thoughts, and frame new questions for further investigation. This can be accomplished through a class discussion after the learners' individual assessments, during the final class period. One of the main points to address is that currently there is no definitive right or wrong answer to "Are we alone in the universe?" That certainly is a drawback and, at the same time, a strength of this investigation, but it is one that I like. Students will learn to use limited evidence to support their view and will need to construct an argument based on what is available, but we, as Earthlings, will have to wait to find out a concrete answer to this essential question.

CONCLUSION

Using the SOURCES framework and primary and secondary sources allows students to explore cross-curricular subjects under one general theme, and in this case, students are able to examine scientific thoughts about extraterrestrial life. Using the *Pale Blue Dot* image and recording as the fundamental sources can create interest and launch an investigation into the consideration of whether we are alone in this universe. The Carl Sagan exhibition on the Library of Congress and NASA websites, as well as others identified in this chapter, are excellent for locating sources related to the possibilities of extraterrestrial life. Their use helps to encourage inquiry-based learning, and they are certainly rich resources for science educators.

QR CODES FOR LINKS IN TEXT

CHAPTER 10

Engaging Students With Emerging Technologies

Web 2.0 Tools for Each of the Stages of the SOURCES Framework

Since the early 2000s, a variety of Internet applications, also known as Web 2.0 tools, have been developed and increasingly have found their way into classrooms. Web 2.0 tools are dynamic web-based applications that have a number of guiding tenets: (a) they are user-friendly, (b) they facilitate a participatory culture, (c) they are system/platform/device-agnostic, and (d) they focus on the integration of user-generated content (Waring & Hartshorne, 2020). Web 2.0 applications and technologies include blogs (e.g., Blogger), wikis (e.g., Wikipedia), media sharing (e.g., YouTube), social networks (e.g., Facebook), social sharing/curation (e.g., Pinterest), social bookmarking (e.g., Digg), and collaborative development tools (e.g., G Suite).

Many of these applications have great potential to support teachers who integrate the use of primary sources into teaching and provide technological aspects, expected by today's student population, into instruction (Hartshorne & Ajjan, 2009). The current generation of students has grown up on the technologies powering computers, tablets, smartphones, and the Internet and has used Web 2.0 applications such as social networks, social bookmarking, media sharing, and mash-ups in their everyday lives; however, modeling and instruction on how to incorporate them into the process of learning and understanding is needed. These and related applications have the potential to enable active participation of students, promote opportunities and environments for reflection, and foster a collaborative and active community of learners, as well as offer multiple pedagogical benefits (Alexander, 2006; Franklin & Van Harmelen, 2007). Many constructivist theorists argue that the use of these Web 2.0 applications in this manner is critical to effective learning and supports the intellectual processes necessary for students to be active and engaged citizens (Ferdig, 2007; Karpf, 2019).

One thing that makes Web 2.0 applications so unique and powerful is that these tools depend on user contributions and interactions as their driving force, provide multiple opportunities for social connectivity and collaborative environments, and are important elements of effective teaching and learning environments. It has been shown that the integration of Web 2.0 tools into instruction holds the potential to improve attitudes toward the learning of content, elevate motivation, increase achievement, and result in a more self-reflective learning environment (Maloney, 2007).

Many believe that the integration of these technologies supports individual growth and development and provides opportunities for students to explore content and problems in new, different, and more authentic ways. Web 2.0 tools provide numerous opportunities for interactions in the learning environment between teachers and students, as well as with more knowledgeable others, such as parents, peers, and subject-matter experts, to effectively and efficiently scaffold student learning.

In this chapter, I will introduce various emerging technologies alongside the SOURCES Framework for Teaching With Primary and Secondary Sources as a way to bolster pedagogical and technological approaches that support active, collaborative, inquiry-based learning. More specifically, the focus of this chapter is on Web 2.0 and emerging technological tools that are effective and appropriate in educational settings and help teachers to more efficiently and authentically integrate the use of primary and secondary sources into instruction. The presentation of these tools will be situated within the various stages of the SOURCES framework.

USING MULTIMEDIA-BASED DISCUSSION AND POLLING TOOLS TO FACILITATE SCRUTINIZING THE FUNDAMENTAL SOURCE(S)

When providing students with opportunities to conduct authentic inquiry and properly moving through the *Scrutinizing Fundamental Sources* stage of the SOURCES framework, teachers need to hook the students' interest with an engaging fundamental source and an essential question for the investigation to come. There are various Web 2.0 tools and resources that can help teachers to provide engaging hooks, as well as supporting critical-thinking strategies, while utilizing technologies of interest to the learner. As with more traditional approaches to discussion, teachers can use Web 2.0 applications such as VoiceThread and Padlet, along with prompts and questions, to engage students with a fundamental source. Integrating additional forms of media into the learning process engenders richer student-driven discussions, deeper and more comprehensive discussion interactions, opportunities to more easily reference online resources, and an improvement of learners' social presence. There also are myriad *polling and surveying tools* available for use in the classroom; one example is Poll Everywhere. These tools can help to engage students as they begin the investigative process and encourage discussion and collaboration. Additionally, these will allow the teacher to access useful data, such as aggregated learner feedback, that can be used as a comparative analysis of an essential question, concept, or collection of primary sources.

VoiceThread

VoiceThread (voicethread.com; Figure 10.1) is a cloud- and multimedia-based discussion board that allows users to easily share audio, video, images, documents, and other media and sources. Other users can interact with the sources posted and comment and respond using audio (via internal microphone, phone, or audio file), text, video (via webcam or external video file), or images/annotations, or a combination of media. Being a cloud-based tool, VoiceThread requires minimal computing power, as content and data are stored and managed on remote servers, rather than on local or personal devices. VoiceThread can be shared with a public or private audience, and the commenting functionality can be controlled by the teacher.

Padlet

Digital bulletin board applications like Padlet (padlet.com; Figure 10.2) are similar to multimedia-based discussion boards such as VoiceThread. However, these possess some important additional functionality. For example, Padlet allows the user to pose essential questions, prompts, resources, or challenges using text, audio, video, images, or web resources. The use of Padlet can

Figure 10.1. VoiceThread Screen Shot

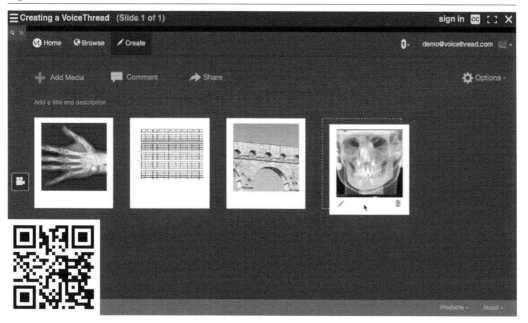

Figure 10.2. Padlet Screen Shot

promote interdependency and interactivity, as this application lets learners develop content in collaboration with others and respond to posts by adding a link to their own self-created Padlet wall or by annotating an existing wall. Padlet's interface and user-friendly features, such as adding various content, moving content, editing content, or even copying content from one Padlet to another, are simple and intuitive. If Padlet is too advanced or time-consuming for this stage of an inquiry, it can be used in later stages, such as the *Establishing a Plausible Narrative* stage.

Poll Everywhere

Digital polls and surveys have a number of pedagogical benefits that align with the disciplined inquiry process promoted throughout the SOURCES framework. The use of polls with students can encourage authentic engagement, increase active learning, provide the teacher with learners' understanding of concepts, and provide learners with agentic empowerment, all of which facilitate more engaged learning environments and support learning. One example is Poll Everywhere (www.polleverywhere.com; Figure 10.3), an extremely flexible and easy-to-use polling/surveying mobile app and/or web-based audience response tool. Through the use of Poll Everywhere, a teacher can collect responses to a multitude of questions, polls, and surveys quickly and easily through student input on a variety of devices. The interface allows for the creation of a variety of open-ended or dichotomous question

Figure 10.3. Poll Everywhere Screen Shot

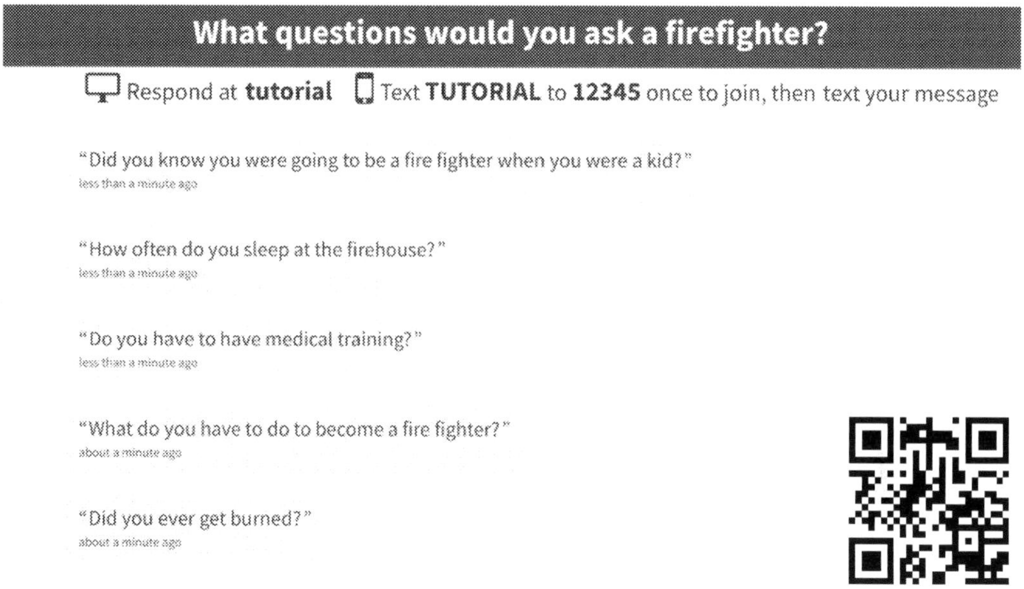

What questions would you ask a firefighter?

💻 Respond at **tutorial**   📱 Text **TUTORIAL** to **12345** once to join, then text your message

"Did you know you were going to be a fire fighter when you were a kid?"
less than a minute ago

"How often do you sleep at the firehouse?"
less than a minute ago

"Do you have to have medical training?"
less than a minute ago

"What do you have to do to become a fire fighter?"
about a minute ago

"Did you ever get burned?"
about a minute ago

formats, provides an assortment of representations of data, and gives the user the ability to export and integrate poll items into PowerPoint, Keynote, or Google Slides presentations, with live responses visible and able to be shared and published in a number of formats.

USING COLLECTION, CATEGORIZATION, STORAGE, AND ANNOTATION TOOLS TO FACILITATE ORGANIZING THOUGHTS

In the second stage (*Organizing Thoughts*) of the SOURCES framework, students are asked to reflect on what knowledge they have at this point in time regarding the fundamental source and the context in which it is situated. They should also consider what questions they have and what additional information is needed, and should begin constructing a plausible response to the essential question. There are a variety of tools that provide the user with ways to critically think about, categorize, organize, annotate, and share primary and secondary sources (e.g., Tizmos, Dropbox, and Google Drive) and create bibliographic reference lists (e.g., Zotero). Additionally, with these tools the teacher can provide various levels of scaffolding for the learners with carefully constructed sets of sources, annotations, and guiding questions. These tools can be used by both teachers and students as mechanisms for enabling learners to progress through the second stage of the SOURCES framework (*Organizing Thoughts*).

Tizmos

Tizmos (www.tizmos.com; Figure 10.4) is a social bookmarking tool that allows the user to create a personalized collection of visual web-based resources, including website addresses and links to videos, images, audio clips, maps, etc. Social bookmarking sites like Tizmos allow for individual or collaborative collection, organization, and sharing of websites. With the registration of a free account, one can create three folders, each of which can hold up to 50 resources; one video-based, rather than still-image-based, Tizmo; and two custom photographs. The visual nature of the Tizmos interface is pleasant and engaging for learners and gives them a visual preview of the resources in an easy-to-use approach. Content can be organized by topic, specific project, date range, or whatever approach that is selected by the teacher or student. With the use of Tizmos, the teacher can provide a structured set of resources that will guide students toward a learning goal rather than send them on possibly aimless searches for content and resources related to the topic of study. Students can create, tag, and share their own Tizmos collections. Other similar social bookmarking sites with functionality related to that of Tizmos include Dropmark (www.dropmark.com[a]) and Pinboard (pinboard.in[b]).

Dropbox and Google Drive

Cloud-based storage sites, such as Dropbox and Google Drive, allow the user to create and share individual or collaborated collections of digital media, text, images, audio, and video. Dropbox (www.dropbox.com; Figure 10.5) is a cloud-based storage service that allows the user to store video, audio, documents,

Figure 10.4. Tizmos Screen Shot

Figure 10.5. Dropbox Screen Shot

images, PDFs, and other file types. The basic free plan provides 2 GB of storage; however, one can obtain additional storage free of charge by recommending users and taking a usability survey. Google Drive (drive.google.com; Figure 10.6) has similar storage functionality but provides a larger amount of free storage (15 GB vs. 2 GB). Both Dropbox and Google Drive can be used for the collection and sharing, by the teacher and students, of individual as well as collaborated collections of primary and secondary sources. With Dropbox and Google Drive, the user can create as many folders as needed, control sharing preferences, and specify levels of interaction (read-only, editing, etc.). These tools can help students organize their thoughts as well as their content, as they move through the stages of the SOURCES framework.

Figure 10.6. Google Drive Screen Shot

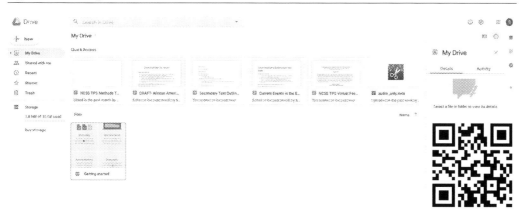

Zotero

Cloud-based bibliographic organization tools have some similarity to social bookmarks and cloud-based storage sites, but these tools focus more on the creation of individual and collaborative collections of bibliographic information for digital resources in various formats. Zotero (www.zotero.org; Figure 10.7) is one that can assist teachers and students in the process of collecting resources, as well as sources, and then organizing, citing, and sharing the collections. With Zotero, the user can import content associated with a resource into the Zotero collection, include notes and attachments, and tag and notate collections and individual resources. For example, a Zotero user viewing a source on the Library of Congress website can easily import the resource and associated metadata into their own collection. For multimedia resources, imported metadata includes item type, title, author, date, URL, tags, notes, and actual images. If a manuscript is added, Zotero will include the title, author(s), abstract, other citation information, tags, and a PDF of the manuscript (if available). The user is thus provided with a full-text searchable collection of sources related to a specific content area, investigation, or essential question. Via a word-processing plugin, Zotero can add citations and automatically create a bibliography based on APA, MLA, Chicago, or other publication styles.

Figure 10.7. Zotero Screen Shot

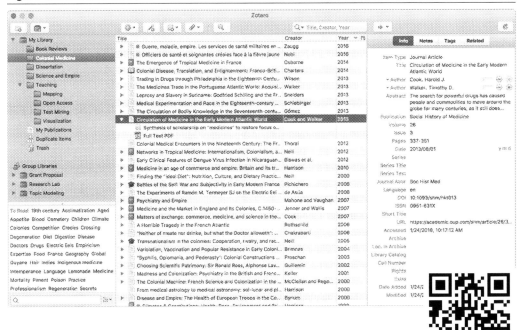

USING COLLABORATIVE AND DISCUSSION TOOLS TO FACILITATE UNDERSTANDING THE CONTEXT

During the *Understanding the Context* stage, students are given an opportunity to strengthen their content knowledge through the analysis and reading of primary and secondary sources. They should think critically about what they know at this point, develop a tentative narrative in response to the essential question, and discern the gaps in their knowledge of the fundamental source and essential question. Teachers can share a variety of secondary sources, but they should also consider the power of utilizing primary sources and associated bibliographic information (author, publisher, abstract, date of creation, etc.) to build upon students' understanding of the specific context associated with the sources and topic being investigated.

YoTeach!, Backchannel Chat, and GoSoapBox

YoTeach! (yoteachapp.com; Figure 10.8), Backchannel Chat (backchannelchat.com; Figure 10.9), and GoSoapBox (www.gosoapbox.com; Figure 10.10) are three backchannel platforms that allow the teacher to survey student knowledge of the content and context associated with the fundamental source and the essential question. These tools permit synchronous (i.e., during class time) and asynchronous (outside of class time) opportunities to gather input from all learners, especially from those who might be less likely to participate in a typical class discussion. These three tools have similar functionality and user interfaces and are fairly easy to use.

Figure 10.8. YoTeach! Screen Shot

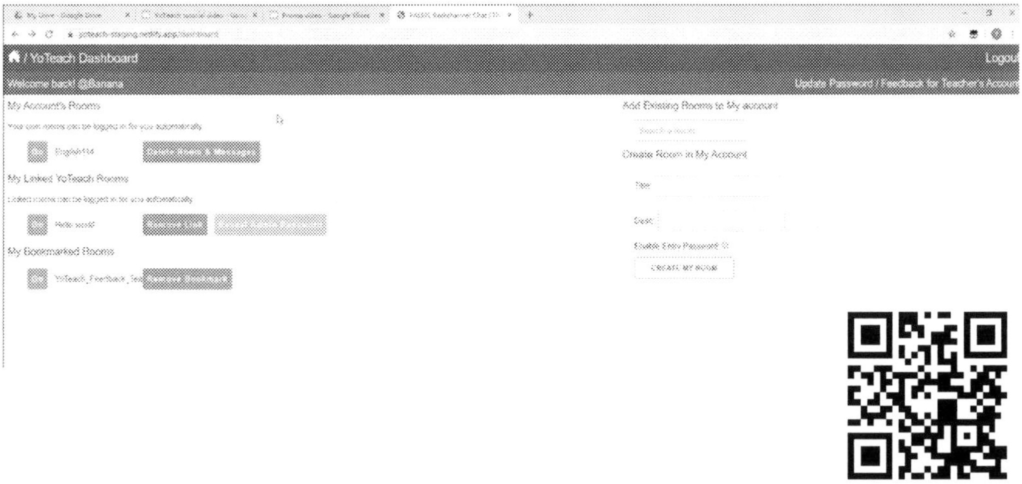

Figure 10.9. Backchannel Chat Screen Shot

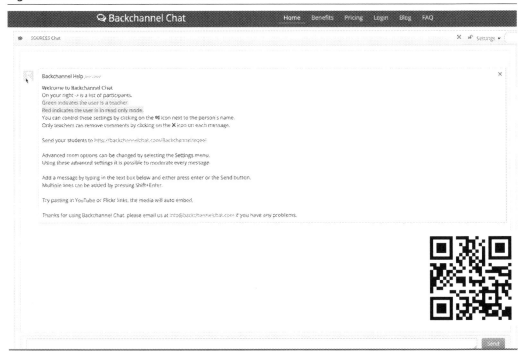

Figure 10.10. GoSoapBox Screen Shot

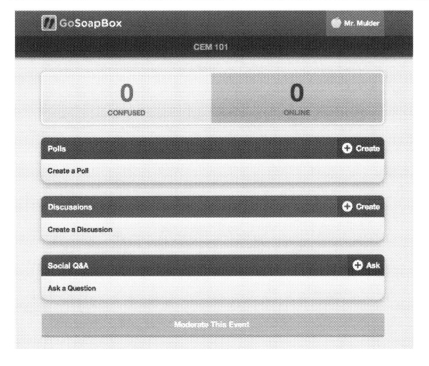

Edmodo

Edmodo (www.edmodo.com; Figure 10.11) is a social networking site similar to Facebook, but it is exclusively used in schools and other educational settings. Teachers can share content and context-related text and resources with students and post primary and secondary sources, links to resources, or prompts to activate their understanding. Through this platform, the instructor can create various environments, facilitate the examination of sources or questions from multiple perspectives, and provide individual groups or the whole class with sources, collections, or other materials via folders. Users can also search the Edmodo network for existing resources, lessons, activities, and challenges. Edmoto can be a useful tool for all phases of the SOURCES framework; however, I have found it to be most useful for the *Understanding the Context* phase.

Figure 10.11. Edmodo Screen Shot

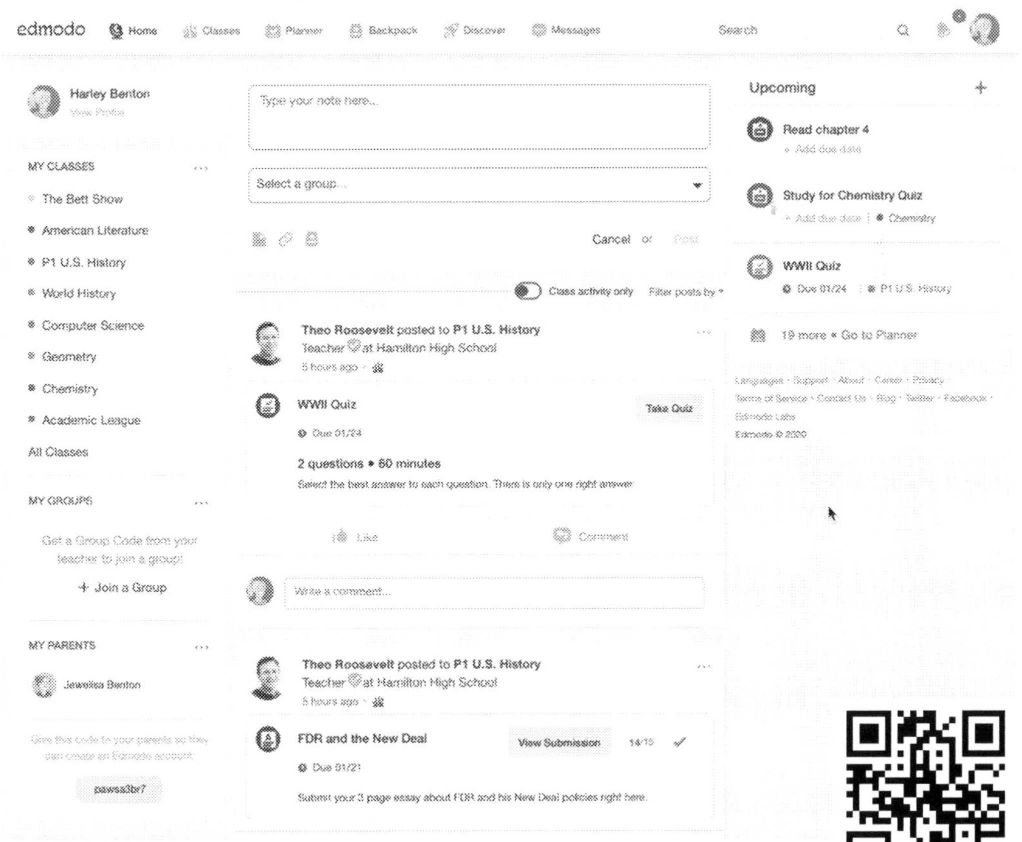

Flipgrid

Flipgrid (info.flipgrid.com; Figure 10.12) is a video discussion tool for educators and students that has a library of topics and resources and the easy familiarity of social media. This tool allows users to post questions and prompts; Flipgrid then provides associated URLs and/or QR codes that will assist students in adding content and context, as well as allow them to provide responses with video, primary sources, or other resources.

USING SCAFFOLDING TOOLS TO FACILITATE
READING BETWEEN THE LINES AND CORROBORATING AND REFUTING

At this point in the investigation, students should have a deeper contextual understanding of the fundamental source and the associated essential question. They are now asked to revisit the fundamental source in the fourth stage (*Reading Between the Lines*) to see how they might engage with and understand

Figure 10.12. Flipgrid Screen Shot

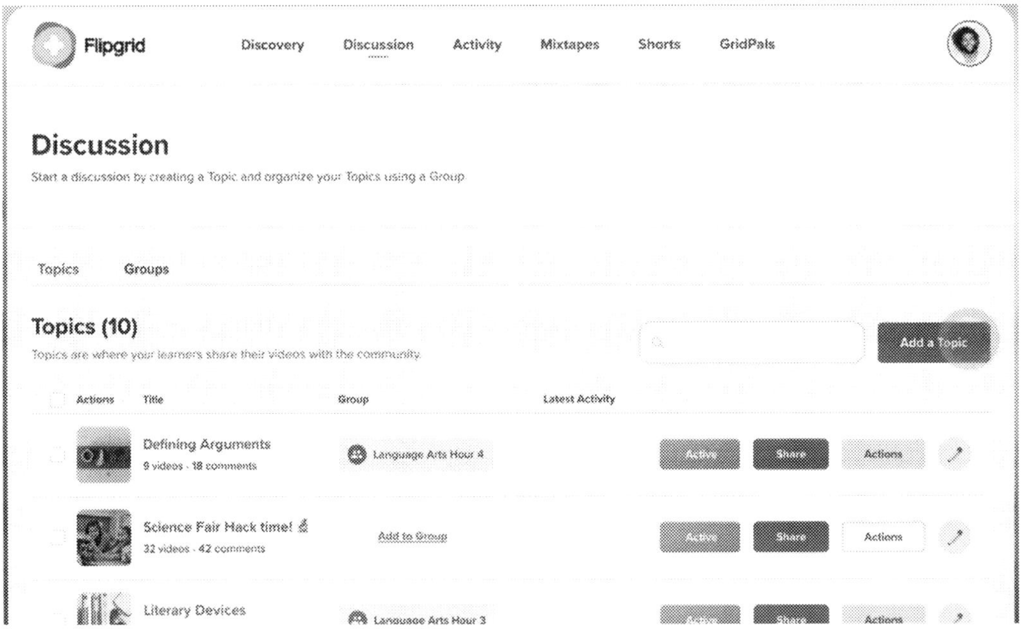

this source differently and how their narrative and questions might have been altered. As they move from this stage into the fifth stage (*Corroborating and Refuting*), students are led to carefully examine a teacher-produced set of primary and secondary sources and/or create one of their own in order to corroborate and refute current understandings about the topic and essential question. This leads them to be able to develop their own plausible narratives in the next stage (*Establishing a Plausible Narrative*). Since these two stages are closely connected, the tools associated with them will be discussed in this section together.

Pear Deck

Pear Deck (www.peardeck.com; Figure 10.13) is a tool that allows educators to develop and share presentations (e.g., PowerPoint, Google Slides) and convert them into more powerful and interactive resources for students. It helps the user create places for students to be able to post and respond to primary and secondary sources or prompts, display content to a controlled group, or manage a large collection of material. Pear Deck presentations provide teachers a place to post sets of sources in a presentation style while allowing students interactivity in the presentations and the ability to respond to questions via text, drawing, and links. Through Pear Deck, the user can also create questions and posts, like Fact and Opinion, Cause and Effect, Name and Purpose for sources, and What Kind of Sources Are These?

Figure 10.13. Pear Deck Screen Shot

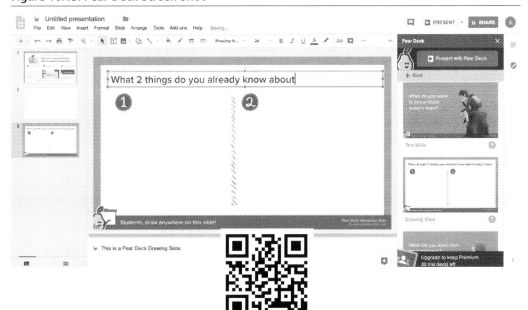

Nearpod

Nearpod (nearpod.com; Figure 10.14) is a tool similar to Pear Deck in that it allows presentations (e.g., PowerPoint, Google Slides) to be converted into interactive resources for learners. An added benefit is that Nearpod works seamlessly with various mobile operating systems, integrates formative assessment functionality, and has greater integration with cloud storage tools such as Dropbox and Box. There are opportunities for additional scaffolding and learner interactivity through the inclusion of audio, drawings, collaborative posts (images and text), three-dimensional elements, open-ended questions, polls, quizzes, embedded slideshows, or video elements. The lessons that are created in Nearpod can be enabled as live lessons or as student-paced lessons, and learners can interact with lessons on desktop or mobile devices.

Biteable

Biteable (app.biteable.com; Figure 10.15) lets teachers create short videos that provide a brief introduction to an investigation, specific guidance or instruction, or additional scaffolding. It can also be used as an assessment tool: Learners produce videos illustrating their conceptual understanding of a essential question or other prompt. In addition to providing an opportunity to create videos from scratch, Biteable has a series of templates available for use and allows for automated rendering of videos, which can be shared instantaneously upon completion of the rendering process.

Figure 10.14. Nearpod Screen Shot

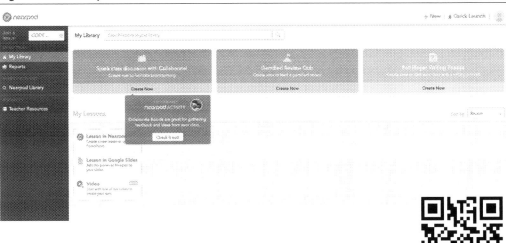

Figure 10.15. Biteable Screen Shot

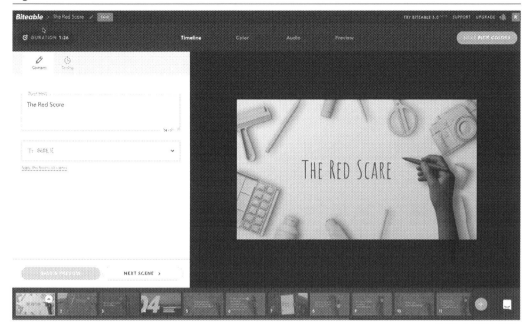

Coggle

Coggle (coggle.it; Figure 10.16) is a collaborative visual concept mapping application that supports individual or collaborative brainstorming. Coggle allows the user to create concept maps, including drag-and-drop functionality, with media from the web, and share them either through a URL or a PDF document. Other useful cloud-based concept mapping tools include MindMup (www.mindmup.com[c]), Bubbl.us (bubbl.us[d]), iMindQ (www.imindq.com[e]), and MindMeister (www.mindmeister.com[f]).

Tes Teach with Blendspace

Tes Teach with Blendspace (www.tes.com/lessons; Figure 10.17) is a browser-based curation tool similar in purpose to Pinterest. Tes Teach with Blendspace lets educators share collections of primary and secondary sources with students, develop innovative and engaging lessons, track student engagement, and integrate web content, YouTube videos, Google Drive content, and other media in an easy manner. Students can also develop collections, modify student- or teacher-created sets, make inferences or provide perspective and viewpoints, and corroborate and refute narratives constructed.

Figure 10.16. Coggle Screen Shot

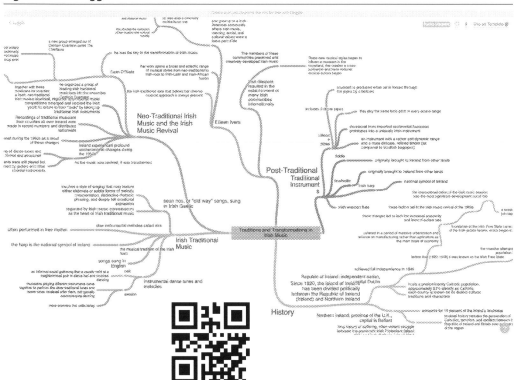

Figure 10.17. Tes Teach With Blendspace Screen Shot

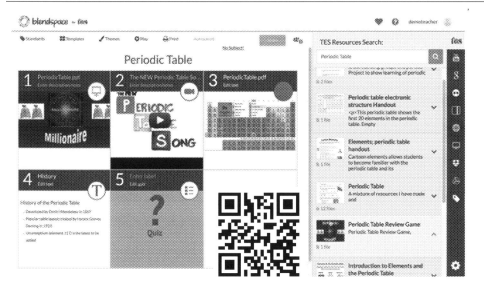

DEVELOPING AND PUBLISHING TOOLS TO FACILITATE ESTABLISHING A PLAUSIBLE NARRATIVE

As students progress through the stages of the SOURCES framework, they will need to construct an original evidence-based narrative, which happens during the sixth stage (*Establishing a Plausible Narrative*). Many emerging technologies can help students construct their own narratives in an authentic and engaging manner and more effectively argue a position and answer the essential question posed at the beginning of the investigation. Narratives can be provided in the form of a traditional paper, but they can also be completed as a documentary video, a website, a diorama, a skit or play, or whatever other form is deemed most appropriate by the teacher. The essential element is that the teacher can properly assess the knowledge obtained by the students and measure how accurately each student responded to the essential question.

Weebly

Weebly (www.weebly.com; Figure 10.18) is an easy-to-use cloud-based website creation and editing service. Users can create up to 10 websites for free. These can be constructed from scratch, but novice users have a choice of templates they can add content to and edit. Additionally, Weebly provides free hosting of Weebly-developed sites (with a web address ending in weebly.com) and offers

Figure 10.18. Weebly Screen Shot

easy linking to an already-owned domain name/web address. Other cloud-based web editors with similar functionality but some distinctions include Wix (www.wix.com[g]) and Google Sites (sites.google.com[h]).

Canva

Canva (canva.com; Figure 10.19) is a wonderful tool to support students during the *Establishing a Plausible Narrative* phase of the SOURCES framework. Canva helps the user demonstrate understanding of a variety of topics through individual or collaborative development of posters, presentations, flyers, infographics, book covers, newsletters, programs, reports, media kits, and more. In addition to the creation of digital artifacts, Canva supports the development of print and physical artifacts.

ThingLink

ThingLink (www.thinglink.com; Figure 10.20) is a browser-based or app-based tool that allows both teachers and students to easily insert "hot spots" into image-based sources. These can be in the form of visible or invisible buttons implanted in a source, and they can be set up to trigger a variety of interactive links, which provides the user a way to greatly expand beyond simply viewing primary and secondary sources. In addition to basic text-based annotation,

Figure 10.19. Canva Screen Shot

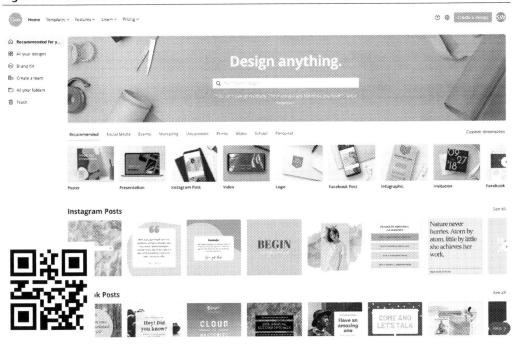

Figure 10.20. ThingLink Screen Shot

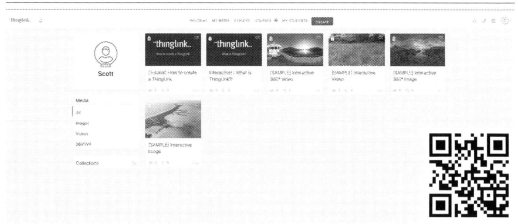

the user can integrate audio or video, embed content from a website, or create a virtual tour with multiple images and interactions. ThingLink provides a unique and engaging approach to the construction of a plausible narrative.

Animoto

Animoto (animoto.com; Figure 10.21) is a video creation site that makes it possible to integrate images, audio, video, text, and other sources easily into user-developed videos of 30 seconds or less. An expert video editor and creator may find Animoto to have limited functionality; however, this site is perfect for educational use, as it gives the learner an easy and effective way to create a plausible narrative without being overwhelmed by too many options and turning the focus of the investigation from the inquiry to the tech tool and its "bells and whistles." Videos can be shared through social media outlets (e.g., Facebook, Instagram, YouTube, Twitter), a URL link, or email, or can be embedded in an existing website.

Explain Everything Whiteboard

Explain Everything Whiteboard (whiteboard.explaineverything.com; Figure 10.22) is a story creator that allows the user to integrate and use audio, video, web resources, and a variety of primary and secondary sources. With Explain Everything Whiteboard, the user can begin a project from a blank slate or utilize a variety of editable templates, such as timelines, Venn diagrams, cause-and-effect diagrams, storyboards, meetings, and notepads. This tool provides the user with various drawing tools and can be used to record and integrate audio. This is another great resource with multiple uses, but it is especially well-suited for the construction of narratives.

Figure 10.21. Animoto Screen Shot

Figure 10.22. Explain Everything Whiteboard Screen Shot

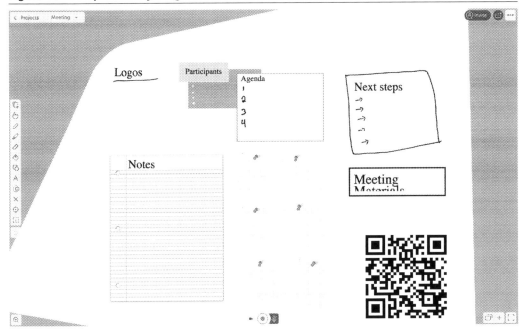

Figure 10.23. Penzu Screen Shot

Penzu

Penzu (penzu.com; Figure 10.23) is a blogging platform that can serve as an online diary or as a personal journal to be shared with the world. Penzu is particularly useful for educational purposes such as this, as it gives students an opportunity to create narratives from scratch and learn how to effectively argue their own plausible narrative. Students can integrate web content such as images, audio, and video seamlessly into their narratives and produce their own personal journal or publication via an automatically generated URL.

CREATING A DIGITAL PORTFOLIO TO FACILITATE SUMMARIZING FINAL THOUGHTS

In the final phase of the SOURCES framework (*Summarizing Final Thoughts*), students are directed to revisit the essential question, the inquiry process used, what was learned regarding the content and how their knowledge was demonstrated, and to critically reflect upon the entire inquiry process and determine how well the process worked for them. Students need to think about how they might modify their approach to inquiry investigations in the future, what scaffolds were and are necessary, if enough perspectives were analyzed, and how the narrative came together. Students need to consider, "How do I know what I know?," "What questions still exist?," and "How might I answer questions that still exist?"

H5P

H5P (h5p.org; Figure 10.24) is an open-source tool for the development, publication, and sharing of diverse interactive content that can be integrated into a number of web-based platforms, including learning management systems like Moodle, Canva, and Blackboard, and content management systems such as WordPress and Drupal. With H5P, users can develop and share interactive videos, presentations, audio recordings, interactive sequences of images, collages, hotspot-infused images, image sequencing, timelines, and virtual tours. Additionally, students can create question-based content,

Figure 10.24. H5P Screen Shot

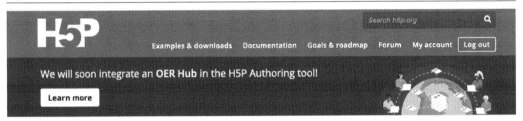

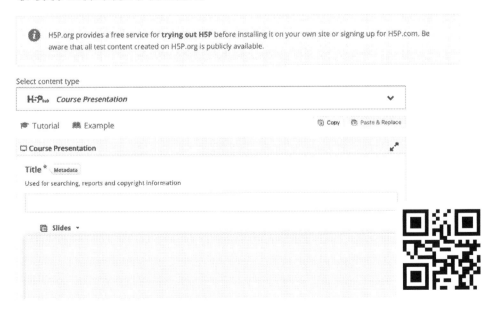

Figure 10.25. Bulb Screen Shot

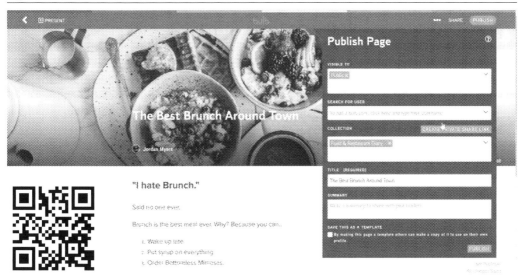

including forms, drag-and-drop tasks/images, image pairing, questionnaires, and image question/answering. One way in which these tools can be used is in an audio reflection journal, in which students record their thoughts and then integrate the journal with other web-based elements and connect it to the learning management system being employed.

Bulb

Bulb (www.bulbapp.com; Figure 10.25) is a browser- and mobile-based tool that helps students develop and share digital portfolios, blogs, and journals. Digital portfolios can be helpful in assessing understanding and learning and in analyzing how the investigative process might be improved in the future. Bulb is easy to use and makes it possible to rank the sources used in order of their importance in responding to the essential question. Students can highlight the areas of their work that ended up being most useful or eye-opening, and reflect on the entire process of investigating the sources and attending to questions.

CONCLUSION

Although many of these tools can be used at various (and possibly all) stages of the SOURCES framework, they were presented in the distinct stages for organizational purposes and as a suggestion for which stage in which they might work best. I know that you will be able to find ways to utilize them far beyond what was briefly described here. Many of these tools can be very powerful when utilized in conjunction with other tools. This will help you to facilitate a richer and deeper learning experience for your students while providing them experience with tools that will make them productive and successful moving forward in their own lives. In the next and final chapter of this book, I will highlight analysis sheets, additional resources, issues to consider, and primary source repositories and resources.

QR CODES FOR LINKS IN TEXT

CHAPTER 11

Additional Resources and Considerations

In this final chapter, I offer additional resources such as analysis sheets and online primary source repositories, consider important factors like image quality and copyright issues, and review the SOURCES Framework for Teaching With Primary and Secondary Sources. The framework, the sources, and the resources provided throughout this book allow educators to consider the potential and possibilities of teaching with primary and secondary sources and emerging technologies and to more energetically and optimistically approach teaching. My hope is that all who read this book can make the most of the inquiry process with their own students.

IMPLEMENTING THE SOURCES FRAMEWORK

Analysis Sheets

As students begin an investigation using the SOURCES framework or analyzing primary and secondary sources, they should be utilizing the SOURCES Analysis Sheet (Figure 1.12) and the SOURCES Framework Analysis Sheet (Figure 1.13). There are also other resources on the Internet that will assist them throughout the inquiry process. Primary-source analysis sheets are vital to the process, especially for novice-level thinkers, so I would suggest the use of the SOURCES Analysis Sheet (Figure 1.12) with the use of any primary or secondary source. Additionally, there are many other options, with many of them providing online PDF versions available for download:

- www.archives.gov/education/lessons/worksheets[a]
- https://www.loc.gov/programs/teachers/getting-started-with-primary-sources/guides[b]
- www.mdhs.org/education/teachers/primary-source-worksheets[c]
- www.calisphere.universityofcalifornia.edu/themed_collections/pdf/6cs_primary_source.pdf[d]

Image Quality and Digital Benefits

To assist students in the process of scrutinizing a primary source in detail, it is vital to provide them with the highest-quality images and media possible, and luckily many of the primary-source repositories are providing high-quality files on their websites. For example, if you were teaching students about late 19th-century America or about how Washington, D.C. has evolved through time, or were looking at different ways to map or depict geographic locations, you might use the image entitled View of Washington City (www.loc.gov/ resource/g3851a.pm001066; Figure 11.1), found on the Library of Congress website. Analyzing the view can be done with a print version of this image; however, when viewing the image directly on the website, students can zoom in (Figure 11.2) and analyze it in greater detail than with a print version alone, as many of the minute details are missed when analyzing the print version.

Figure 11.1. View of Washington City

Figure 11.2. Zoomed Section of View of Washington City

PRIMARY SOURCES AND COPYRIGHT

Although it typically is not of the utmost concern, it is important to remember that when students are using primary sources in the construction of assessments and projects, they should be mindful not to break copyright law. To better inform students about copyright, one can begin by viewing a short video (Teacher Resource: Copyright Quick Check) found on the Library of Congress's website (www.loc.gov/item/webcast-6804[c]). Other resources that can be helpful when talking about copyright are the Cornell Law School website (www.law.cornell.edu/uscode/text/17/110[f]) and the U.S. Copyright Office website (www.copyright.gov/help/faq/faq-fairuse.html[g]). These help educators and students better understand Section 110 of the copyright statute, which addresses copyright exemptions and rights that apply to display of materials in nonprofit and educational settings, both physical and digital. Further, as stated by the experts at the Library of Congress, the user should consider three questions prior to the distribution or use of a source, as a single "yes" to any of these questions means that you probably will not need to conduct a fair-use evaluation:

1. Will I just link to this primary source, instead of reproducing it?
2. Was this primary source published before 1924?
3. Was this primary source created by U.S. federal employees as part of their job?

Although you may determine that the answer to a question is yes, you should still always check the rights and reproduction statements associated with any sources that are to be reproduced or disseminated, as one may learn that there are restrictions on use of the item that are not immediately clear.

If the answer is no, then the individual wishing to use the source must conduct her own assessment of its "fair use." Although the language defining fair use may not be clear to everyone, the determining factors are listed in Section 107 of the statute, here italicized and followed by further information from the U.S. Copyright Office:

- *Purpose and character of the use, including whether the use is of a commercial nature or is for nonprofit educational purposes*: Courts look at how the party claiming fair use is using the copyrighted work, and are more likely to find that nonprofit educational and noncommercial uses are fair. This does not mean, however, that all nonprofit education and noncommercial uses are fair and all commercial uses are not fair; instead, courts will balance the purpose and character of the use against the other factors below. Additionally, "transformative" uses are more likely to be considered fair. Transformative uses are those that add something new, with a further purpose or different character, and do not substitute for the original use of the work.
- *Nature of the copyrighted work*: This factor analyzes the degree to which the work that was used relates to copyright's purpose of encouraging creative expression. Thus, using a more creative or imaginative work (such as a novel, movie, or song) is less likely to support a claim of a fair use than using a factual work (such as a technical article or news item). In addition, use of an unpublished work is less likely to be considered fair.
- *Amount and substantiality of the portion used in relation to the copyrighted work as a whole*: Under this factor, courts look at both the quantity and quality of the copyrighted material that was used. If the use includes a large portion of the copyrighted work, fair use is less likely to be found; if the use employs only a small amount of copyrighted material, fair use is more likely. That said, some courts have found use of an entire work to be fair under certain circumstances. And in other contexts, using even a small amount of a copyrighted work

was determined not to be fair because the selection was an important part—or the "heart"—of the work.

- *Effect of the use upon the potential market for or value of the copyrighted work*: Here, courts review whether, and to what extent, the unlicensed use harms the existing or future market for the copyright owner's original work. In assessing this factor, courts consider whether the use is hurting the current market for the original work (for example, by displacing sales of the original) and/or whether the use could cause substantial harm if it were to become widespread. (United States Copyright Office, 2019, para. 2)

You can learn more about copyright basics from the U.S. Copyright Office or through their site outlining "What does copyright protect?" (www.copyright.gov/help/faq/faq-protect.html[h]). The University of Minnesota's site for "Thinking Through Fair Use" (www.lib.umn.edu/copyright/fairthoughts[i]) can be quite helpful for educators determining fair use in their classroom.

PRIMARY SOURCE REPOSITORIES AND RESOURCES

There are numerous locations for finding primary and secondary sources for use in the classroom, as well as sites that provide resources for teachers and students. Here are a few I have found particularly useful.

Library of Congress

The Library of Congress (www.loc.gov[j]) is the largest library in the world. Luckily, efforts have been made to digitize many sources found in its collections, so one can find tens of millions of books, recordings, photographs, newspapers, maps, manuscripts, and other sources on the library's website. The Library of Congress is the main research arm of the U.S. Congress and the home of the U.S. Copyright Office. Although there are many sections of the website that would be of interest to many educators, one of the most valuable is the one dedicated to education. In the Teachers section of the website, the user can find information on classroom materials, professional development, using primary sources, and other topics. I would suggest taking a look at the Classroom Materials section, as there are premade primary sources sets, lesson plans, presentations, and classroom-based activities provided there. The primary sources sets can easily be modified for use with the SOURCES Framework for Teaching With Primary and Secondary Sources. Although these resources are extremely helpful, keep in mind that there are millions of other sources available through general searches or browsing the collections.

Educational Projects Supported by the Library of Congress

The following are projects that have been funded through the Library of Congress's initiative Teaching with Primary Sources. They are terrific resources for extending the learning and inquiry process and for finding additional primary sources.

DBQuest (www.icivics.org/products/dbquest[k]) is a site that introduces students to major questions in civics and history through the use of primary sources and necessitates the use of evidence in the process of answering "Big Questions." A Big Question acts as a guiding light for deep examination of three selected primary resources. Each document challenges students to dig into the text itself and find the relevant information through document-based supporting questions and helps to get students writing strong arguments based on evidence.

Case Maker (mycasemaker.org[l]) is a customizable system for inquiry-based learning for 6–8 students using primary sources from the Library of Congress. Modeled after the "observe, reflect, question" framework developed under the Teaching with Primary Sources program, Case Maker guides students to review a challenge question, collect evidence, and make a case.

Eagle Eye Citizen (www.eagleeyecitizen.org[m]) engages middle and high school students in solving and creating interactive challenges on American history, civics, and government with Library of Congress primary sources in order to develop students' civic understanding and critical-thinking skills.

Engaging Congress (engagingcongress.org[n]) is a series of game-based learning activities that explores the basic tenets of representative government and the challenges that it faces in contemporary society. Primary-source documents are used to examine the history and evolution of issues that confront Congress today.

KidCitizen (www.kidcitizen.net[o]) introduces a new way for young students (K–5) to engage with history through primary sources. In KidCitizen's nine interactive episodes, children explore civics and government concepts by investigating primary-source photographs from the Library of Congress. They also connect what they find with their daily lives. KidCitizen includes cloud software tools that let educators create their own episodes and share them with students.

National Archives and Records Administration

The National Archives and Records Administration (NARA; www.archives.gov) was established in 1934 by President Franklin Roosevelt and is considered the record keeper of the United States. Its major holdings date from 1775 and include a:

sweep of the past: slave ship manifests and the Emancipation Proclamation; captured German records and the Japanese surrender documents from World War II; journals of polar expeditions and photographs of Dust Bowl farmers; Indian treaties making transitory promises; and a richly bound document bearing the bold signature "Bonaparte"—the Louisiana Purchase Treaty that doubled the territory of the young republic. (National Archives and Records Administration, n.d., para. 5)

The sources that NARA keeps are those considered to have "continuing value." These sources number around 10 billion pages of text, 12 million maps, charts, and drawings, 25 million photographs and graphics, 24 million aerial photographs, 300,000 reels of motion picture film, 400,000 video and sound recordings, and 133 terabytes of electronic data. A wide variety of items can be found on the website (www.archives.gov[p]), so the user should take time to search and browse this amazing resource. However, for teachers, one of the most valuable areas of the NARA website is the Educator Resources section, which includes DocsTeach (www.docsteach.org[q]). DocsTeach was made for classroom use and has excellent ready-to-use activities, digital versions of important sources, and tools that can assist students in analyzing sources and thinking critically. One of the most valuable educational projects of NARA is the Our Documents initiative (www.ourdocuments.gov[r]). This site examines the top 100 milestone documents of the United States, so teachers can access digital versions of the Lee Resolution (1776) to the Voting Rights Act (1965) when teaching about the history of our nation.

Smithsonian Institution

The Smithsonian Institution, founded in 1846 with funds donated by James Smithson (1765–1829), is the world's largest museum, education, and research complex. Its goal is to shape "the future by preserving our heritage, discovering new knowledge, and sharing our resources with the world" (Smithsonian Institution, n.d., para. 1). The Explore & Learn section of the website (www.si.edu[s]) provides a variety of sources, resources, activities, and research tools for teachers and students. In the Smithsonian Learning Lab (learninglab.si.edu[t]), students can find more than one million resources, create personal collections and educational experiences, and share their creations and work.

University Repositories and Projects

Various universities throughout the United States have online repositories of primary and secondary sources, as well as educational and research-based resources for visitors to their sites. I suggest that you search the many university-based repositories and projects focused on teaching and learning with primary sources. For an example of a university repository, the University of North Carolina's Documenting the American South (DocSouth) is a digital publishing initiative (docsouth.unc.edu[u]) that provides access to texts, images, and audio files related to Southern history, literature, and culture. Among the many collections, the First-Person Narratives of the American South (docsouth.unc.edu/fpn[v]) offers many Southerners' perspectives on their lives by presenting letters, memoirs, autobiographies and other writings by slaves, laborers, women, aristocrats, soldiers, and officers. One university-based site that includes sources as well as instructional approaches and resources is the Stanford History Education Group's (SHEG) website (sheg.stanford.edu[w]). SHEG seeks to improve education by conducting research, working with school districts, and reaching directly into classrooms with free materials for teachers and students. The Reading Like a Historian curriculum (sheg.stanford.edu/history-lessons[x]) has been created to engage students in authentic inquiry. Each lesson revolves around a central critical question and features a set of primary documents designed for groups of students with a range of reading skills.

eBay and Other Online Auctions

One type of resource that may not immediately come to mind in a search for unique primary sources is the online auction site, e.g., eBay (www.ebay.com[y]). For those not familiar with online auctions, they are somewhat similar to face-to-face auctions for selling items ranging from antiques to sports collectibles to electronics to cars and homes. Educators might not think of online auctions as resources, but many offerings there pertain to the content covered in K–12 classrooms. The items available for sale open opportunities for utilizing primary sources and exposing students to multiple perspectives, as well as allowing them to see cultural artifacts from all over the world that they otherwise might never have the opportunity to see.

Similar to the marketing of a home, sellers create an advertisement of the item for sale, which includes a title, description, picture(s) of the item, location of the seller, starting price, and shipping and handling charges. As with items being auctioned in a traditional format, a beginning bid price is set, as well as a timetable for the duration of the auction. Users are able to submit a single bid or a maximum bid, or may have an opportunity to buy the item at a desired price preset by the seller.

One important thing that users should be aware of prior to purchasing anything through an online auction site is the seller's ratings and shipping and handling charges. Buyers are encouraged to provide details of their buying experience, so as a potential buyer, you should review some of the previous transactions of the seller and look at the seller's rating and number of positive and negative reviews. Many of the sellers are quite knowledgeable about the items that they sell, are antique dealers, and have done some research prior to purchasing the item themselves. As with any purchase, buyers must beware and should carefully read the transaction stipulations, in order to protect themselves and be sure that the item for sale is what is expected. Sellers typically welcome questions from the potential buyer, so you should feel free to contact them to clarify any questions about the item for sale prior to purchase.

School budgets for purchasing instructional materials are often minimal or nonexistent, so educators may want to use online auctions as electronic resources for bolstering their own knowledge about a topic of study or for printing the images of the items for sale there, as they are typically quite clear and of high quality. The descriptions can help create background or supplemental information for teachers and, depending on their age, for students as well. Educators can select the image posted for an item for sale and save them for printing and for use in a variety of ways.

One area on the eBay site that can be quite useful is the Collectibles & Art section. Within the Collectibles & Art Section, one can choose a subsection entitled Collectibles. In the Collectibles section, items for sale are categorized within subgroups, such as comics, sci-fi and horror, photographic images, advertising, ethnic and cultural, and historical memorabilia, all ranging from pre-1700 to the present day. One area that I have found to be useful is the one related to the home front in the United States during the Second World War. For example, when searching eBay for items related to the American home front during the Second World War, one can start with Collectibles and follow links to arrive eventually at Original WW II US Home Front Collectibles (www.ebay.com/b/Original-WW-II-US-Home-Front-Collectibles/4723/bn _3123821?rt=nc&_sop=16; Figure 11.3). This section typically has anywhere from 8,000 to 15,000 items for sale at any one time. As this is a continually updated auction, the offerings can be different each time a visitor comes to the site. Perusing the American home front catalogue one can find ration stamp books, magazines, letters, diaries, photo albums, advertisements, posters, war bonds booklets, and other ephemera. Once again, one could choose to save or print the images rather than purchasing them, if funds were not available for this purpose, and thus, I enjoy searching by highest-price item first to see what items are available, even if not affordable.

SOURCES FRAMEWORK FOR TEACHING WITH PRIMARY AND SECONDARY SOURCES

As demonstrated throughout the book, the SOURCES Framework for Teaching With Primary and Secondary Sources, the SOURCES Analysis Sheet (Figure 1.12), and the SOURCES Framework Analysis Sheet (Figure 1.13) were developed to give students a structured way to utilize primary and secondary sources in an authentic discipline inquiry-based approach to learning about

Figure 11.3. eBay Section for Items From the American Home Front During World War II

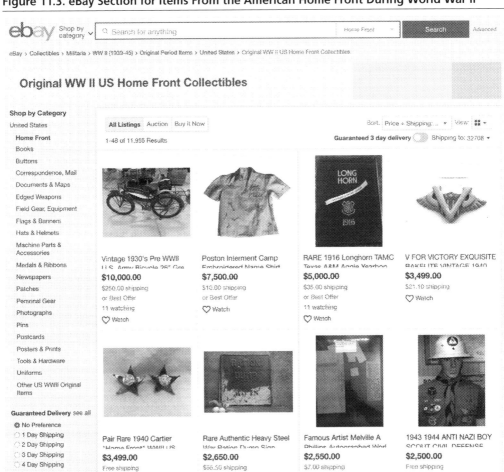

content across all areas. Through the seven stages of the SOURCES framework, the students' learning process is carefully planned and scaffolded in order to allow each individual opportunities to examine primary and secondary sources, question their understandings about a topic, event, or subject, develop background knowledge, find supporting and corroborating evidence, construct source-based narratives, and critically analyze the learning process and findings, as well as consider questions that were not answered.

I argue that not only do students need the critical-thinking skills necessary to progress through the seven stages of the SOURCES framework, it is essential that they have opportunities to engage with primary and secondary sources in authentic ways while utilizing the technologies of today and the future. These are all key elements to becoming more engaged and participatory citizens in a democracy. This is why I determined that, through the production of this book, I would demonstrate the power of the SOURCES Framework for Teaching With Primary and Secondary Sources and show how teachers can utilize emerging technological applications, alongside the SOURCES framework, to empower students, provide agentic and critical-thinking opportunities, and creatively extend instructional approaches.

> **The SOURCES Framework for Teaching With Primary and Secondary Sources**
>
> 1. Scrutinizing the Fundamental Source(s)
> 2. Organizing Thoughts
> 3. Understanding the Context
> 4. Reading Between the Lines
> 5. Corroborating and Refuting
> 6. Establishing a Plausible Narrative
> 7. Summarizing Final Thoughts

THE FUTURE, POSSIBILITIES, POTENTIAL ROADBLOCKS, AND MAKING THE MOST OF THE INQUIRY PROCESS

Over the past 20 years or so, the availability of and accessibility to a wide variety of primary and secondary sources has greatly increased. Where once a teacher would have to purchase primary source kits or visit a museum or library to access primary and secondary sources, there are now billions of sources available in a matter of moments. The struggle, for many, has been how to properly integrate these sources, as well as the plethora of emerging technologies, into the classroom in a seamless, authentic, and engaging manner. Through the pedagogical approaches, the SOURCES framework, and resources provided in this book, I hope that I have empowered educators, in all content areas, with the knowledge and desire to authentically challenge and engage the minds of students in classrooms across the country and beyond. As a reminder, I welcome emails (scott.waring@ucf.edu[z]) and future discussions about what you find here in the book and on the Teaching with SOURCES website (www.teachingwithsources.com[aa]). The skills gained in the process of engaging with primary and secondary sources through the use of the SOURCES Framework for Teaching With Primary and Secondary Sources and the use of emerging technologies gives students the power to be productive, informed, and engaged citizens in the ever-changing and complex world around them.

QR CODES FOR LINKS IN TEXT

z. aa.

References

Alexander, B. (2006). A new way of innovation for teaching and learning. *EDUCAUSE Review, 41*(2), 32–44.

All-American Girls Professional Baseball League. (n.d.). *League history.* www.aagpbl.org /history/league-history

Allen, J. (1994). If this is history, why isn't it boring? In S. Steffy & W. J. Hood (Eds.), *If this is social studies, why isn't it boring?* (pp. 1–12). Stenhouse.

Apfeldorf, M. (2018, March 20). *Mathematics and primary sources: Historic codes, ciphers, and computational thinking, Part I.* Library of Congress. blogs.loc.gov/teachers/2018/03 /mathematics-and-primary-sources-historic-codes-ciphers-and-computational-thinking-part-i/?loclr=blogtea

Barnett, J. H., Lodder, J., & Pengelley, D. (2016). Teaching and learning mathematics from primary historical sources. *PRIMUS, 26*(1), 1–18.

Barton, K. C. (2005). Primary sources in history: Breaking through the myths. *Phi Delta Kappan, 86*(10), 745–753.

Barton, K. C., & Levstik, L. S. (2003). Why don't more history teachers engage students in interpretation? *Social Education, 67*(6), 358–361.

Bickford, J. H., Clabough, J., & Taylor, T. N. (2020). Fourth-graders' reading, thinking, and writing about historical sources. *Social Studies Research and Practice, 15*(1), 57–82.

Black, M. S., & Blake, M. E. (2001). Knitting local history together: Collaborating to construct curriculum. *Social Studies, 92*, 243–247.

Boaler, J. (2002). *Experiencing school mathematics: Traditional and reform approaches to teaching and their impact on student learning.* Routledge.

Britt, J., & Howe, M. (2014). Developing a vision for the Common Core classroom: What does elementary social studies look like? *Social Studies, 105*(3), 158–163.

Callison, D. (2013). CCSS: Primary sources for secondary social studies. *School Library Monthly, 30*(2), 18–21.

Cattaneo, K. H. (2017). Telling active learning pedagogies apart: From theory to practice. *Journal of New Approaches in Educational Research, 6*(2), 144–152.

Costa, T., & Doyle, B. (2004). Runaway slave advertisements: Teaching from primary documents. *Middle Level Learning, 20*, 4–9.

Cowgill, D., & Waring, S. M. (2015). Using SOURCES to examine the American Constitution and events leading to its construction. *The Councilor: A Journal of the Social Studies, 76*(2), 1–14.

Cummings, R. D. (2019). Justice then and now: Engaging students in critical thinking about justice and history. *The Social Studies, 110*(6), 281-292.

Danner, R. B., & Musa, R. (2019). Evaluation of methods teachers use in teaching Shakespearean drama in senior secondary schools in Edo State. *Journal of Teaching and Teacher Education, 7*(2).

Ellis, J. J. (2004). *His excellency: George Washington.* Alfred A. Knopf.

Faraon, M., Jaff, A., Nepomuceno, L. P., & Villavicencio, V. (2020). Fake news and aggregated credibility: Conceptualizing a co-creative medium for evaluation of sources online. *International Journal of Ambient Computing and Intelligence, 11*(4), 1–25.

Ferdig, R. E. (2007). Examining social software in teacher education. *Journal of Technology and Teacher Education, 15*(1), 5–10.

Fischer, D. H. (2004). *Washington's crossing: Pivotal moments in American history.* Oxford University Press.

Franklin, T., & Van Harmelen, M. (2007). *Web 2.0 for content for learning and teaching in higher education.* Joint Information Systems Committee. https://www.google.com/url?sa=t&rct=j&q=&esrc=s&source=web&cd=&ved=2ahUKEwjdoKHatd_rAhUuw1kKHR2pB_4QFjABegQIAxAC&url=http%3A%2F%2Fstaff.blog.ui.ac.id%2Fharrybs%2Ffiles%2F2008%2F10%2Fweb-2-for-content-for-learning-and-teaching-in-higher-education.pdf&usg=AOvVaw1rHj2gr1CNgRH9MwcPooDW

Frassanito, W. (1975). *Gettysburg: A journey in time.* Scribner.

Hancock, J. (1777, January 6–7). *To George Washington from John Hancock, 6–7 January 1777.* founders.archives.gov/documents/Washington/03-08-02-0002

Hartshorne, R., & Ajjan, H. (2009). Examining student decisions to adopt Web 2.0 technologies: Theory and empirical tests. *Journal of Computing in Higher Education, 21*(3), 183–198.

Herlihy, C., & Waring, S. M. (2015). Using the SOURCES framework to examine the Little Rock Nine. *Oregon Journal of the Social Studies, 3*(2), 44–51.

Hoyer, J. (2020). Out of the archives and into the streets: Teaching with primary sources to cultivate civic engagement. *Journal of Contemporary Archival Studies, 7*(1), Article 9.

Karpf, D. (2019). *The Internet and Engaged Citizenship, Circa 2019.* American Academy of Arts and Sciences. www.amacad.org/publication/internet-and-engaged-citizenship/section/3.

Ketchum, R. M. (1973). *The winter soldiers: The battles for Trenton and Princeton.* Henry Holt and Company.

Knox, H. (1777, January 7). *Letter to Lucy Knox.* www.gilderlehrman.org/collection/glc0243700514

Lamb, A. (2014). Primary source digital documents: CCSS & complexity of text. *School Library Monthly, 30*(4), 5–8.

LaVallee, C., Purdin, T., & Waring, S. M. (2019). Civil liberties, the Bill of Rights, and SOURCES: Engaging students in the past in order to prepare citizens of the future. In J. Hubbard (Ed.), *Extending the ground of public confidence: Teaching civil liberties in K–16 social studies education* (pp. 3–32). Information Age Publishing.

LaVallee, C., & Waring, S. M. (2015). Using SOURCES to examine the *Nadir of Race Relations* (1890–1920). *The Clearing House, 88,* 133–139.

Lawrence, S. A., Langan, E., & Maurer, J. (2019). Using primary sources in content areas to increase disciplinary literacy instruction. *The Language and Literacy Spectrum, 29*(1), 1–18.

Lewis, D. (2016, May 25). *An archive of fugitive slave ads sheds new light on lost histories: Wanted ads posted by slave owners reveal details of life under slavery*. Smithsonian Magazine. www.smithsonianmag.com/smart-news/archive-fugitive-slave-ads-could-shed-new-light-lost-histories-180959194

Library of Congress. (n.d.). *How to get into Princeton* [Video file]. www.loc.gov/item/myloc19

Library of Congress. (2019). *Using primary sources*. www.loc.gov/teachers/usingprimarysources

Maloney, E. (2007). What Web 2.0 can teach us about learning. *The Chronicle of Higher Education, 25*(18), B26.

Maloney, W. (2018). *Japanese-America's pastime: Baseball*. Library of Congress Blog. blogs.loc.gov/loc/2018/05/japanese-americas-pastime-baseball

McGrew, S., Ortega, T., Breakstone, J., & Wineburg, S. (2017). The challenge that"s bigger than fake news: Civic reasoning in a social media environment. *American Educator, 41*(3), 4–9.

McLean, S., Attardi, S. M., Faden, L., & Goldszmidt, M. (2016). Flipped classrooms and student learning: Not just surface gains. *Advances in Physiology Education, 40*(1), 47–55.

Mora, R. (2011). "School is so boring": High-stakes testing and boredom at an urban middle school. *Penn GSE Perspectives on Urban Education, 9*(1), 1–9.

National Archives and Records Administration. (n.d.). *About the National Archives of the United States*. www.archives.gov/publications/general-info-leaflets/1-about-archives.html

National Council for the Social Studies. (1994). *Expectations of excellence: Curriculum standards for social studies*. www.socialstudies.org/standards/stitle.html

National Council for the Social Studies. (2010). *National curriculum standards for social studies: A framework for teaching, learning, and assessment*. Author. https://www.socialstudies.org/standards/national-curriculum-standards-social-studies

National Council for the Social Studies. (2013). *The college, career, and civic life (C3) framework for social studies state standards: Guidance for enhancing the rigor of K–12 civics, economics, geography, and history*. Author. https://www.socialstudies.org/standards/c3

National Governors Association Center for Best Practices and Council of Chief State School Officers. (2010). *Common core state standards*. Author. http://www.corestandards.org

Sergeant R_____. (1896). The Battle of Princeton. *The Pennsylvania Magazine of History and Biography, 20*(4), 515–519.

Singer, A. J. (2007). Venture Smith's autobiography and runaway ad: Enslavement in early New York. *Middle Level Learning, 28*, 2–7.

Smithsonian Institution. (n.d.). *About the Smithsonian*. www.si.edu/about

Stryker, W. S. (1898). *The battles of Trenton and Princeton*. The Riverside Press.

Sullivan, T. (1908). The Battle of Princeton. *The Pennsylvania Magazine of History and Biography, 32*, 54–57.

Tanner, H. S. (1816). Affair of Princeton. In James Wilkinson (Ed.), *Diagrams and plans illustrative of the principal battles and military affairs treated of in memoirs of my own times*. Abraham Small.

Terry, K., & Waring, S. M. (2017). Expanding historical narratives: Using SOURCES to assess the successes and failures of Operation Anthropoid. *Social Studies Journal, 37*(2), 59–71.

Thomas, A. (2020). Sources and citizens: An essay in applied epistemology. *Policy Futures in Education, 18*(4), 531–544.

Unal, Z., & Unal, A. (2017). Comparison of student performance, student perception, and teacher satisfaction with traditional versus flipped classroom models. *International Journal of Instruction, 10*(4), 145–164.

United States Bureau of the Census. (1975). *Historical statistics of the United States, colonial times to 1970: Part 1.* www.census.gov/history/pdf/histstats-colonial-1970.pdf

United States Copyright Office. (n.d.). *What does copyright protect?* www.copyright.gov/help/faq/faq-protect.html

United States Copyright Office. (2019). *More information on Fair Use.* www.copyright.gov/fair-use/more-info.html

Wang, T. P. (2007). The comparison of the difficulties between cooperative learning and traditional teaching methods in college English teachers. *The Journal of Human Resource and Adult Learning, 3*(2), 23-30.

Waring, S. M. (2015). Asking students to compare the value of information presented in different sources about the same event. *Social Education, 79*(1), 6–10.

Waring, S. M. (2016). Teaching with primary sources: Moving from professional development to a model of professional learning. In T. Petty, A. Good, & S. M. Putman (Eds.), *Handbook of Research on Professional Development for Quality Teaching and Learning* (pp. 295–306). IGI Global.

Waring, S. M. (2017). Engaging history students through the use of the SOURCES Framework. *In Context, 1*(1), 2–4.

Waring, S. M. (2019). Framing historical thinking in the digital age. In T. Heafner, R. Hartshorne, & R. Thripp. (Eds.), *Handbook of research on emerging practices and methods for K–12 online and blended learning* (pp. 436–458). IGI Global.

Waring, S. M., & Hartshorne, R. (2020). *Conducting authentic historical inquiry: Engaging learners with SOURCES and emerging technologies.* Teachers College Press.

Waring, S. M., & Herlihy, C. (2015). Are we alone in the universe? Using primary sources to address a fundamental question. *The Science Teacher, 82*(7), 63–66.

Waring, S. M., LaVallee, C., & Purdin, T. (2018). The power of agentic women and SOURCES. *Social Studies Research and Practice, 13*(2), 270–278.

Waring, S. M., & Scheiner-Fisher, C. (2014). Using SOURCES to allow digital natives to explore the Lewis and Clark expedition. *Middle School Journal, 45*(4), 3–12.

Waring, S. M., & Tapia-Moreno, D. (2015). Examining the conditions of Andersonville Prison through the use of SOURCES. *The Social Studies, 106*(4), 170–177.

Washington, G. (1776, December 20). *George Washington to Continental Congress.* www.loc.gov/resource/mgw3a.002/?sp=117

Washington, G. (1776, December 27). *From George Washington to Robert Morris.* founders.archives.gov/documents/Washington/03-07-02-0357

Washington, G. (1777, January 5). *From George Washington to Major General Israel Putnam, 5 January 1777.* founders.archives.gov/documents/Washington/03-07-02-0416

Watson, J. (2017). *Famous codes and ciphers through history and their role in modern encryption*. www.comparitech.com/blog/information-security/famous-codes-and-ciphers-through-history-and-their-role-in-modern-encryption

Wertenbaker, T. J. (1922). The Battle of Princeton. In *The Princeton Battle Monument: The history of the monument, a record of the ceremonies attending its unveiling, and an account of the Battle of Princeton*. Princeton University Press.

White, S. H., O'Brien, J. E., Smith, A., Mortensen, D., & Hileman, K. (2006). A history lab environment in the classroom brings the standards to life. *Middle School Journal, 37*(4), 4–10.

Wineburg, S. (2010). Historical thinking: Memorizing facts and stuff? *Teaching with Primary Sources Quarterly, 3*(1), 2–4.

Wolff, M., Wagner, M. J., Poznanski, S., Schiller, J., & Santen, S. (2015). Not another boring lecture: Engaging learners with active learning techniques. *The Journal of Emergency Medicine, 48*(1), 85–93.

Wooten, D., Clabough, J., & Blackstock, E. (2019). Elementary students socially construct their own historically-grounded wordless picture books. *The Councilor: A Journal of the Social Studies, 80*(2), 1–10.

Woyshner, C. (2010). Inquiry teaching with primary source documents: An iterative approach. *Social Studies Research and Practice, 5*(3), 36–45.

Zakaria, E., & Syamaun, M. (2017). The effect of realistic mathematics education approach on students' achievement and attitudes towards mathematics. *Mathematics Education Trends and Research, 2017*(1), 32–40.

Zhao, Y., & Hoge, J. D. (2005). What elementary students and teachers say about social studies. *The Social Studies, 96*, 216–221.

Index

About the Author

Scott M. Waring is a professor and the program coordinator for the Social Science Education Program at the University of Central Florida. He earned his bachelor's and master's degrees in Education from the University of South Florida and his PhD from the University of Virginia in Social Studies Education, with a minor in Instructional Technology. He teaches courses at the undergraduate and graduate level in social science methodology, research, and theory. While at the University of Central Florida, Dr. Waring has won the Award for Excellence in Research, the Excellence in Graduate Teaching Award, the Excellence in Undergraduate Teaching Award, the Excellence in Academic Advising Award, and the Award for Excellence in Undergraduate Academic Advising. He is the current chair of the Teacher Education and Professional Development Committee of the National Council for the Social Studies (NCSS), chair of the Florida College and University Faculty Assembly (FLCUFA—the higher education research affiliate of the Florida Council for the Social Studies), and the program chair for the SOURCES Conference. Dr. Waring serves as the editor for *Social Studies and the Young Learner*, editor for *Teaching with Primary Sources Journal*, and the interdisciplinary feature editor for *Social Studies Research and Practice*. He has served as a member of the National Council for the Social Studies (NCSS) House of Delegates, on the Executive Board for the College and University Faculty Assembly (CUFA—the higher education research affiliate of NCSS), as the editor for *Contemporary Issues in Technology and Teacher Education—Social Studies*, and as the chair for the Society for Information Technology & Teacher Education's (SITE) Social Studies Special Interest Group. He has delivered more than 100 conference and workshop presentations and has written or cowritten grants and awards totaling more than $4 million, including a Teaching with Primary Sources grant from the Library of Congress, a Fulbright-Hays grant (Czech Republic), a Fulbright Specialist Award (Bulgaria), a Fulbright Scholar Award (Czech Republic), and three United States Department of Education Teaching American History grants. Dr. Waring has published three books (and has two edited books in progress), multiple journal articles, and book chapters focusing on the teaching and learning of history, teaching with primary sources, and the utilization of technology in teaching.